Mary for Protestants

Mary for Protestants

*A Catholic's Reflection on
the Meaning of Mary the Mother of God*

R. DIVOZZO

RESOURCE *Publications* • Eugene, Oregon

MARY FOR PROTESTANTS
A Catholic's Reflection on the Meaning of Mary the Mother of God

Copyright © 2019 Richard J. Divozzo. All rights reserved. Except for brief quotations in critical publications or reviews, no part of this book may be reproduced in any manner without prior written permission from the publisher. Write: Permissions, Wipf and Stock Publishers, 199 W. 8th Ave., Suite 3, Eugene, OR 97401.

Resource Publications
An Imprint of Wipf and Stock Publishers
199 W. 8th Ave., Suite 3
Eugene, OR 97401

www.wipfandstock.com

PAPERBACK ISBN: 978-1-5326-7583-6
HARDCOVER ISBN: 978-1-5326-7584-3
EBOOK ISBN: 978-1-5326-7585-0

Manufactured in the U.S.A.   MAY 1, 2019

I wish to dedicate this book to our Lady, the triumph of whose Immaculate Heart I hope this book will help bring about in the heart of every Christian to the honor and glory of Our Lord Jesus Christ and the reign of His Most Sacred Heart.

Truly, you are blessed among women. For you have changed Eve's curse into a blessing; and Adam, who hitherto lay under a curse, has been blessed because of you. Truly, you are blessed among women. Through you the Father's blessing has shone forth on mankind, setting them free of their ancient curse. Truly, you are blessed among women, because through you your forebears have found salvation. For you were to give birth to the Savior who was to win them salvation. Truly, you are blessed among women, for without seed you have borne, as your fruit, him who bestows blessings on the whole world and redeems it from that curse that made it sprout thorns. Truly, you are blessed among women, because, though a woman by nature, you will become, in reality, God's mother. If he whom you are to bear is truly God made flesh, then rightly do we call you God's mother. For you have truly given birth to God.

—FROM THE LITTLE OFFICE OF THE BLESSED VIRGIN MARY

Contents

Acknowledgments / ix

1 What's the Meaning of This? / 1
2 Mary, the Mother of God / 7
3 Mary and Her Immaculate Conception / 11
4 Mary and the Life of Jesus / 22
5 Mary's Visitation to Elizabeth / 25
6 Mary as the Ark of the New Covenant / 32
7 Mary and the Birth of Jesus / 39
8 The "Purification" of Mary and the Dedication of Jesus / 43
9 Mary Loses Jesus in Jerusalem / 47
10 Mary and the Wedding at Cana / 51
11 Mary and the Passion of Christ / 58
12 Mary at the Cross / 63
13 Mary and the Resurrection / 69
14 Mary and the Mystery of the Ascension / 77
15 Mary at Pentecost, the Descent of the Holy Spirit / 81
16 The Assumption and Coronation of Mary / 87
17 The Meaning of Mary's Virginity / 94
18 Mary's Past / 100

Epilogue / 105
Appendix A / 113
Appendix B / 122
Bibliography / 125

Acknowledgments

I WOULD LIKE TO thank my good friends, Steve Ayers and Mark Pestana, for their invaluable help in reading the manuscript and recommending corrections and improvements.

1

What's the Meaning of This?

THIS LITTLE BOOK IS an attempt to present to the orthodox believing Protestant the Catholic understanding and appreciation of Mary, the Mother of our Lord Jesus Christ. As a Protestant convert to the Catholic Church, I remember my own misgivings before conversion about even the little I knew of Catholic teaching on the Blessed Virgin and would hope that others might have an advantage I didn't have. It would be truer to say, rather than "misgivings", that I had scarcely any understanding of Mary at all. I had hardly given her a thought. She was little more to me than a commonplace figure on Christmas cards, an object of sentiment at a sentimental time of year. She had nothing to do with my understanding of the Faith. Of course, as an orthodox Evangelical Christian, I accepted her virginity, at least so far as the birth of our Lord was concerned, but beyond that she was to me and to most of my co-religionists in the Evangelical tradition at most just one of many wheels in the exquisite machinery of God's salvific plan, an ordinary woman given to do an extraordinary thing, but no different from (indeed, of much less importance than) the Apostles or anyone else through whom God worked miracles or communicated the Gospel. Had I reflected (even a little) on Mary's participation in God's plan of salvation as the "handmaid of the Lord", her role in the scheme of the Redemption would have seemed to me so much richer and more profound than the understanding of it I received from the tradition in which I was raised. I might have begun to understand the significance of the fact of her *voluntary* participation in God's plan: "Let it be done to me according to Your word"—her *"fiat"* ("let it be") as it is expressed to in the Latin Catholic tradition. I might have begun to appreciate what Scripture actually tells us about Mary. Admittedly, there is very little about her *explicitly*—if, that is, one is merely counting "verses". But there is much more about Mary in Scripture that is clearly implicit and which is hard to ignore if you're *interested*.

I want to impress upon my reader two things about Mary which may at first glance seem contradictory. First, that Mary is unique in the sinlessness of her immaculate soul, having been preserved at conception from Original Sin to bear the incarnate God. And second, that she is also a redeemed soul who like us partakes of divine grace for her salvation through the redemptive Sacrifice of Christ. Mary is not a demi-goddess, still less the presumptive fourth person of the Eternal Godhead. Her glory is conferred, not inherent.

This book is not intended to be an argument for the Catholic doctrine of Mary, although it will necessarily involve some argument to clear away misunderstanding about her. It is rather intended to be a reflection on her that is informed by Catholic doctrine. I make no apology for the terms used that seem to the Protestant to beg the question. This book is meant to be a sort of invitation to consider Mary to those of a theological tradition that have largely ignored her. Therefore, the terms used, which are born of a two-thousand-year-old tradition of thought about her, are necessary. Of course, the Protestant might say that there are good reasons to largely ignore her as Mary has no special theological status. So, whatever arguments are advanced here are meant not to overwhelm, but to indicate forcefully that she *deserves* the consideration she has been denied her by modern Protestants, who have broken with a long tradition which even their forerunners respected.

It may surprise many Evangelical Protestants especially that John Calvin said of Mary, "It cannot be denied that God in choosing and destining Mary to be the Mother of his Son, granted her the highest honor."[1] And the great Swiss Reformed theologian, Ulrich Zwingli, said of Mary, "The more the honor and love of Christ increases among men, so much the esteem and honor given to Mary should grow"[2]. John Wycliffe, the pre-Lutheran reformer of the later Middle Ages honored Mary in one of his sermons: "It seems to me impossible that we should obtain the reward of Heaven without the help of Mary. There is no sex or age, no rank or position, of anyone in the whole human race, which has no need to call for the help of the Holy Virgin."[3] Even Luther, it is generally agreed, despite his opposition to much of Roman Catholic teaching, continued to honor Mary long after his revolt from the Church. Theologians appear to agree that Luther adhered to the Marian decrees of the ecumenical councils and dogmas of the Church. He held fast to the belief that Mary was a perpetual virgin and the *Theotokos* ("God-bearer") or Mother of God: "It is an article of faith that Mary is Mother of the Lord and still a Virgin."[4] Special attention is given to the assertion, that Luther some three-hundred years before the dogmatization of the Immaculate Conception by Pope Pius IX in 1854, was a firm adherent of that view. Others maintain that Luther in later years changed his position on the Immaculate Conception, which, at that time was undefined (and therefore not a dogma) in the Church, maintaining however the sinlessness of Mary throughout her life, adhering to the Marian decrees of the ecumenical councils of the Church and maintained that Mary remained sinless throughout her life. But it is clear that Luther's veneration of Mary informed his preaching and teaching:

> Mary is the Mother of Jesus and the Mother of all of us even though it was Christ alone who reposed on her knees . . . If he is ours, we ought to be in his situation;

1. Calvin, *Calvini Opera*, vol. 45, 348.
2. Zwingli, *Zwingli Opera, Corpus Reformatorum*, vol.1, 427-428.
3. "Devotion to the Blessed Virgin Mary," *Catholic Encyclopedia*.
4. Luther, *Martin Luther's Works*, Vol. 11, 319-320.

there where he is, we ought also to be and all that he has ought to be ours, and his mother is also our mother." (Sermon, Christmas, 1529) No woman is like you. You are more than Eve or Sarah, blessed above all nobility, wisdom, and sanctity. (Sermon, Feast of the Visitation. 1537) One should honor Mary as she herself wished and as she expressed it in the Magnificat. She praised God for his deeds. How then can we praise her? The true honor of Mary is the honor of God, the praise of God's grace. Mary is nothing for the sake of herself, but for the sake of Christ . . . Mary does not wish that we come to her, but through her to God. (Explanation of the Magnificat, 1521).

Luther's veneration of Mary flowed from a Christocentric theology as it does in Catholic theology, although he mistakenly believed that "Papists" worship Mary, blurring the line between admiration and idolatry. Even so, he could say of her, "Men have crowded all her glory into a single phrase: The Mother of God. No one can say anything greater of her, though he had as many tongues as there are leaves on the trees."[5]

John Calvin accepted the veneration of Mary but in a strictly qualified sense. He was far from indifferent to Mary as the Mother of our Lord, but wanted to free her from what he considered undeserved "Papist" titles and honors which were due only to Jesus Christ. Like Luther, Calvin misunderstood Mary's status in Catholic doctrine, supposing that the Church taught that Mary had no need of redemption, which was and remains untrue of Catholic teaching, and that she needed God's grace as much as any other human being, which was true and which the Church—if Calvin had only known it—had always believed. Like Luther, Calvin misunderstood Catholic veneration of Mary as "Queen of Heaven" to be adoration. It is worth noting here that Catholic veneration (the Greek word is *douleia*) pays that honor due someone whom God Himself has already honored; adoration in Catholic doctrine is something different in kind and is reserved for God alone (the Greek word is *latreia*). In their own way, Protestants, according to

5. Luther, *Luther's Works*, vol. 22, 23.

their respective traditions, venerate Luther or Calvin, that is to say they honor them. They have great historical significance and are believed to have been great servants of God, from whose services through the grace of God have bestowed great benefits on (at least) the Christians who followed them.

Despite this kind of veneration of their own, the Protestant Christian has the tendency to make of the order of grace and thus of Christ's Church and heaven an egalitarian affair, as if sanctification is strictly uniform and knows no distinctions between souls, each being equally holy before God. No one, in this way of thinking, grows closer to God than anyone else; or, if anyone does, it makes no difference in heaven. The assumption seems to be that what we do in this life, at least so far as grace is concerned, is irrelevant to what we enjoy in the next. Of course, no orthodox Christian really believes this as a point of doctrine. Otherwise, a holy life is of no consequence to how God will finally judge us. Of course, the Church has always taught what most Protestants have always insisted on, that absolutely no one could ever stand up to God's judgment without first having received His sanctifying grace (the Pelagian heresy was condemned by the Council of Carthage in 418) and even those will require His mercy, for *all have sinned and fallen short of the glory of God* (Rom. 3:23). Mary received His saving grace too; only she received it before she was born, at her conception. In the womb she could not have consented to her salvation, but shall we admonish God for dispensing His grace as He pleases? But, to be sure, it was only by the grace she received at her first moment of existence that Mary was able to cooperate so thoroughly and intimately as she did (and still does in her exalted place in Heaven) in her quiet, unobtrusive, meditative way ("and she pondered all of these things in her heart"; "and a sword shall pierce your heart also"), with God's work of salvation. There is no salvation for anyone outside the grace of God; nor is there any *effective* grace without our cooperation with it. Both conditions are the demands of love. Yet the objection to Mary's special honor, that she should be thought to be above all others in the order of God's grace, implies a kind of democracy of grace, which ignores any distinction of the various degrees to which God's goodness actually obtains among Christians.

Karl Barth, the great Swiss theologian of the Reformed Tradition, who considered the Roman Catholic veneration of Mary "a terrible mistake and heresy", still more than his predecessors, could not appreciate Mary beyond the bare credal statements about her. He could not see (or could not accept) the idea that Mary (or anyone) could occupy the highest place in God's salvific plan; He supposed that in the order of grace that there is Jesus at the top as the One Who dispenses grace and immediately below Him is a vast undifferentiated mass of the redeemed who receive it.

It is evident, then, that the early Protestants respected and honored Mary and this tendency (though qualified) to honor her was subsequently lost. It was for the early Protestants a question of the kind and degree of honor to give her. How is she to be honored and regarded, being the virgin mother of Jesus? Is her role in God's work of redemption a mystery to be plumbed by the profoundest contemplation or only an (albeit) prime miracle to be accepted by faith and left at that?

2

Mary, the Mother of God

SHOULD ANYONE OUTSIDE THE Catholic tradition, take an interest in Mary apart from her being simply the mother of Jesus? The answer (and the premise of this book) is, of course, "Yes", because she is *necessarily* (as I hope to show) the Mother of God, the one chosen to be the means by which God would in the Person of Jesus Christ take on our human nature in order to reveal Himself to us and redeem us. All orthodox Christians confess that Mary is at very least the vehicle of the Incarnation. But ought we to think of her as anything more than an ignorant but virtuous Jewish girl in ancient Palestine chosen by God as if at random from a number of other possible virgin females of her race and time capable of bearing children, to bear the God-Man, the Savior of the world? Again, the answer is an emphatic "Yes". There is a great deal to be said of the fact that Mary was the means, the *willing* agent, by whom God would redeem the world in His Son. She is, as she declared herself at the Annunciation, the Handmaid of the Lord.

An inexorable logic obtains when one begins to reflect carefully on Mary as the Mother of God. The expression, Mother of God, (*"theotokos"*—"God-bearer", a favorite of the Greek ante-Nicene Fathers), may make many present-day orthodox Protestants uneasy, but what the phrase expresses is the inescapable truth about Mary. If she gave birth to Jesus Christ, Who is, as all true Christians profess, both God and man, then it necessarily follows that Mary is in *fact* (not only in doctrine) the *Theotokos*, the Mother of God. Many Protestants object to calling her by that title, because it glorifies her, presumably at the expense of our Lord Himself. And indeed it does glorify her, but not at Christ's expense. The appellation glorifies her, not because it expresses a fond sentiment about Mary, still less because of a heretical exaggeration of her importance, that distracts one's devotion from Christ Himself, but because that title expresses what she *is* by God's own act, the one by whose agency He revealed Himself to the world. Calling Mary the Mother of God, therefore, expresses a belief that is at the root of our faith in Jesus Christ Himself, that by realizing His incarnate life as the son of Mary, she has become the human agency of God's Incarnation.

Mary thus is involved *by God's own doing* in the act and meaning of His incarnation. And such depths of her own meaning to us must be carefully plumbed. The glory Mary obtains as the Mother of God is then hers only because God Himself has so glorified her as He will glorify everyone who remains in Christ. "*And the glory which thou hast given me, I have given to them; that they may be one, as we also are one: I in them, and thou in me; that they may be made perfect in one: and the world may know that thou hast sent me, and hast loved them, as thou hast also loved me*" (John 17:23-5). Mary is simply the first and greatest of all human beings to be so glorified. Mary only shares by grace the glory that, truly, belongs only to Jesus Christ and has been His from all eternity in His eternal Godhead.

It may be objected too, as many Protestants do, that the claim for Mary to be the Mother of God is unbiblical as there is no specific biblical text in which that title is attributed to her and thus to attribute to Mary that honor is to claim for her what Scripture does not sanction. But is it really the case that Scripture does not sanction the title, even while Scripture nowhere specifically mentions it? How else but from Scripture itself do we know of Mary and her role in the Incarnation: her humble acceptance at the archangel's

Annunciation; the joy she expressed at being chosen to bear God's Son at the Visitation to her cousin Elizabeth, who when she saw Mary proclaimed, "Blessed are you among women, and blessed is the fruit of your womb! And why is this granted me, that the *mother of my Lord* should come to me?", and then Mary's actually giving birth to the divine Child? It is only from Scripture that we know anything of this or that it was Mary herself who bore Jesus, just as we know from Scripture alone that He is the Incarnate God. As that is the case and as the title "Mother of God" professes at once the fact of both Jesus' divinity and of Mary's bearing Him into the world, it simply follows that, far from contradicting the Scripture, to honor Mary as the Mother of God is perfectly consonant with it and with our faith as Christians. The honor, then, does not originate, as many otherwise orthodox Protestants believe, in a medieval Catholic spirituality that had lost all touch with what the early Church believed and which thereby elevated Mary beyond her purely, unqualified human role to somewhere on the same level with Jesus Himself. This honor due Mary was bestowed on her by God Himself by virtue of choosing her to bear His Son into the world. Nothing could be more natural or inevitable than to honor Mary by recognizing this most obvious fact about her.

The reasoning above is very simple, as simple as the classic syllogism of Logic 101: All men are human; Socrates is a man; therefore, Socrates is human. Jesus is God; Mary bore Jesus (Who also grew in her womb for nine months in the course of normal gestation); therefore, Mary is God's Mother. It could not be simpler to understand. Those who cannot *believe* it, however, because, as many Fundamentalist Protestants have argued, they think it is not possible that God should have a real human Mother as it contradicts the doctrine of the Holy Trinity and His absolute being, these might for the same reason also deny the Incarnation itself, which in the same way defies all reason. If, against all rational probability, the Second Person of the Blessed Trinity can become fully human and still fully retain His divine nature as God the Son, what would have prevented Him from taking a woman to be His Mother? It does not violate His absolute, uncontingent Being or His divine nature any more than His taking on human nature does. At very least, it is no less believable.

Indeed, to deny the fact of Mary being the Mother of God is to deny the full humanity of Christ. It's the old Monophysite heresy or a version of it called *dyophysitism*, which was condemned at the Council of Chalcedon (451) and maintains that Christ acquired His divine nature *after* His birth. But if you believe, as all orthodox Protestants do, that Jesus was from *conception* at once wholly God and wholly man and if you also accept the divine inspiration of the Scripture in its account of Mary as the human agency of God's becoming a man, then there is no conceivable reason not to *call* her what all Christians called her up until and long after the Reformation and what she plainly *is*, the Mother of God.

3

Mary and Her Immaculate Conception

IT MAY SURPRISE MOST Protestants that the Catholic doctrine of Mary's Immaculate Conception also follows from the Incarnation. Again, a little reflection on what this doctrine means may demonstrate its unassailable orthodoxy to those who find it untenable as contrary to the true Christian Faith. With the intention of keeping these reflections clear and simple, I will avoid any discussion of the doctrine's more obscure complexities and keep along broad lines to indicate the fundamental truth of the teaching. There are great depths here for the theologian and the mystic, but for the plain Christian and for our purposes, it is best to keep to the idea or doctrine in its simplicity.

The Immaculate Conception has to do with Mary as the human agency of God's Incarnation. God descended from Heaven into the world, but He did so *through* the womb of a virgin. This mode of descent was, again, God's choice, not Mary's or anyone else's. It was simply announced to Mary and she cooperated with God's intentions for her. Her cooperation, while necessary and exalting, is not why the Catholic Church calls her "most holy" (an attribution that is, of course, relative to all other human beings, not to God). What makes her "most holy" is that she was free of original sin. The question to ask that is most to the point about such a claim is not, How can anyone other than Jesus Christ Himself be free of original sin?, but rather, How could God have been *naturally* born of a woman *unless* she was free of original sin?

It might conceivably have been that original sin since Adam's Fall is freshly imputed by God to every soul at conception; but no one in or out of the Church has ever taught such an idea before or after the Reformation. And, of course, it has always been clearly out of the question that the Redeemer should have been born of a woman who had been born in sin like every other woman. Rather, the clear force of all the evidence from Scripture and from the Church Fathers on this point is that original sin is naturally transmitted by human generation. original sin is passed on, one might say, genetically. Of course, it won't be found on any strain of DNA any more than one could find Jesus' divine nature written on His genetic code; it's not after all a specifically biological component but a quality of the soul necessarily infected by Adam's sin.

Adam being the first of the human race was necessarily the progenitor of everyone who came after him, because we came *from* him. So, biological propagation is evidently the means of the transmission of Original Sin. Saint Paul calls Jesus the "Last Adam" or the "Second Man" Who came to restore to the human race what (at least) we lost in the Fall. If we accept the testimony of the Church Fathers and of the whole Christian Tradition until the 16th century, it follows that if our Lord was the Second Adam, then Mary, by her cooperation in the redemption of mankind, is the Second Eve. She is to Christ what Eve was to Adam, a partner or "helpmate like unto himself" (Gen. 2:18), someone to help Him in the *regeneration* of Man. As Eve by her disobedience cooperated in the Fall of man, so Mary, by her obedience at the Annunciation in freely accepting her role as the Christ-bearer, cooperated in man's redemption.

The Adam/Christ parallel certainly has the explicit sanction of the Scriptures and the Apostolic authority of St. Paul; but the Mary/Eve parallel is no less clear from what is implied by the witness of the Holy Scriptures. The Fathers of the Church, steeped as they were in the Scriptures, are themselves a clear witness to this parallelism. John Henry Newman, the great scholar and Catholic convert, who was himself persuaded by the testimony of the Fathers concerning Mary as the Second Eve, had demonstrated the Fathers' unmistakable confidence in Mary's role as the "New Eve" in a chapter in his *Extracts for the Times*. I won't reproduce here his long list of citations of the Fathers[1] which runs to several pages, but Newman's long list of patristic testimony (with his commentary) from at least the second century to the sixth makes clear and certain the early Church's express belief, "the rudimental view," as he called it, in the role of Mary as the Second or New Eve. St Jerome (347-420) neatly sums up the Fathers' love and veneration of Mary with the expression, "Death by Eve, life by Mary," (Epistle 22). And note Newman's comment on testimony of the Fathers:

> ... at the time of their sentence, an event was announced for the future, in which the three same parties were to meet again, the serpent, the woman, and the man; but it was to be a second Adam and a second Eve, and the new Eve was to be the mother of the new Adam. "I will put enmity between thee and the woman, and between thy seed and her seed." The Seed of the woman is the Word Incarnate, and the Woman, whose seed or son He is, is His mother Mary. This interpretation, and the parallelism it involves, seem to me undeniable; but at all events (and this is my point) the parallelism is the doctrine of the Fathers, from the earliest times; and, this being established, we are able, by the position and office of Eve in our fall, to determine the position and office of Mary in our restoration.[2]

We have seen how commonplace in the writings of the Fathers is the regard for Mary as the "Second Eve". Mary's obedient reception of God's will at the Annunciation was not only the antithesis of Eve's disobedience, it was the beginning of its *reversal*, God's great work of undoing the Fall, which we call the Redemption of Man. The parallels between Mary and Eve are hard to miss when

---

1. Newman, *Mary: The Second Eve*. See Appendix A.
2. Newman, *Mary: The Second Eve*.

we consider how both were unique in being situated in history at the genesis of creation (Mary at the inception of the "new creation" in Christ). The contrast between them more than anything else highlights Mary and Eve's parallel significance in the God's plan of redemption: Eve's disobedience of God began the misery of the human race; Mary's obedience brought about the promise and possibility of our eternal happiness. It is interesting to note as well each woman's emotional response to the respective angels (Satan and Gabriel) that spoke to them. It is an exquisite irony that Eve was "all ears" itching at the outrageous proposition Satan was suavely making to her; and Mary's very different response: she was, we are told, (at first) "troubled" at the Gabriel's astonishing announcement that God had chosen her for this glorious role. Mary in simple trust obeys God's will in spite of her inability to comprehend it or its messenger. Eve, on the other hand, is lulled into presumption and disobedience by the Serpent's sweet reason. Each woman acted at a pivotal moment in human and cosmic history, on which turned (respectively) the Fall of the human race and the triumph of God's Love.

When St. Justin Martyr (died. c. 165) made what is known to be the earliest reference to the Eve/Mary parallel, he was probably referring to an older tradition. Here is what he wrote contrasting the Annunciation to Mary with Eve's temptation in the Garden:

> [The Son of God] became man through a Virgin, so that the disobedience caused by the serpent might be destroyed in the same way it had begun. For Eve, who was virgin and undefiled, gave birth to disobedience and death after listening to the serpent's words. But the Virgin Mary conceived faith and joy; for when the angel Gabriel brought her the glad tidings that the Holy Spirit would come upon her and that the power of the Most High would overshadow her, so that the Holy One born of her would be the Son of God, she answered, 'Let it be done to me according to thy word' (Lk. 1:38). Thus was born of her the [Child] about whom so many Scriptures speak, as we have shown. Through Him, God crushed

the serpent, along with those angels and men who had become like the serpent.[3]

There is no doubt that the Incarnation, God's "taking manhood into Himself" (to use St. Athanasius' phrase), is at the center of the Christian Faith. But if so, neither can there be any reasonable doubt that Mary, the woman in whose womb the Incarnation occurred, acquires by that fact a unique role in the whole of history. The question for Protestant Christians is whether or not Mary's role in God's Redemption of man goes beyond her carrying our Lord to term and raising Him as any good mother would. But that question will be answered in the course of this book, for the great importance of Mary as the Mother of God is not merely historical but also ineluctably theological and as such pertains to the spiritual life of everyone who loves her Son. At this point, however, I want only to establish why the Fathers of the Church avidly celebrated Mary as the Second Eve. Her obedience to God at the Annunciation (her "*fiat*" or "let it be" or her "Yes" to God) began the unraveling of the disastrous effects of Eve's disobedience in the Garden. This unraveling, of course, only Christ Himself could accomplish; but Mary's humble, cooperative participation in it made her the first person, the premier actor, to share God's glory in His redemptive act. The Catholic Church venerates her saints and martyrs because of their unwavering faithfulness to God, and it is because of Mary's unerring faithfulness to God's will with her immaculate soul that she was the first and most deserving of all mankind to receive such veneration. Mary's honor is thus the reward and hope of every faithful Christian. Hers is certainly the greatest honor for hers is the greatest perfection by virtue of her being made at conception free of original sin. But her perfection is not different in kind, only in degree from what we all may hope for and all by Christ are called to ("Be perfect as your Father in heaven is perfect."—Mat. 5:18). Mary is called in the Roman Rite of the Mass by a phrase the Church has always interpreted as alluding to her, taken from the Book of Judith in the Old Testament, "the

---

3. Gambero, *Mary and the Fathers of the Church*, 47.

highest honor of our race". And so did the angel Gabriel call her "blessed among women".

The angel Gabriel also called her "full of grace", which the Church has always understood to mean a declaration of Mary's absolute purity of soul as being in full possession of the divine grace lost through original sin at the Fall. Many of the newer translations of the Bible render the phrase in the passage of St. Luke's Gospel 1:28 as "highly favored". Any theological debate over Mary's status with respect to Original Sin must begin with the textual question of what exactly were the words spoken to Mary by Gabriel at the Annunciation. Gabriel is either saying Mary is full of "grace" with all that that most laden of all theological words (which includes the idea of favor but in the Catholic tradition much more) implies; or, he is simply respectfully doffing the hat, so to speak, and paying the lady the courtesy of acknowledging her status as someone to whom God is paying His special attentions.

Many who defend the "favored" translation place a great deal of importance on the fact that "full of grace" is not directly from the Greek text but is a translation of the Latin of St. Jerome's Vulgate text, *plena gratia*. They would point out that "full of grace" appears in the Greek in two other verses, but not this one.

The word at issue is the Greek *kecharitōmenē*, at the root of which is the verb *charitoō*, from which comes the English word *charisma*. The stock New Testament Greek word for "grace" is *charis*, the companion noun of *charitoō*. Admittedly, *kecharitōmenē* is a unique use of the word, and so difficult to translate. Many modern translators of the Bible, prefer to render *Charis* as "favor" and so *kecharitōmenē* becomes "highly favored"; earlier translations, such as the Authorized Version or the King James Bible, once the favored translation among orthodox Protestants, renders it "grace" 132 times out of 156 instances of the word. Only 7 of them does it translate as "favor". Although there is nothing wrong theologically with the modern rendering, it is the weaker of the two expressions, "highly favored" and "full of grace"; and there appears to be no reason *not* to render *charis* as "grace", especially as it has historically been the preferred one even in expressly Protestant translations.

We may then assume that "favor" is not the normal *theological* sense of *charis* since *charitoo* and *kecharitōmenē* are defined in *Vine's Expository Dictionary of New Testament Words* and *Thayer's Greek Lexicon* as well as other (Protestant) lexicographical sources as being principally related to the theological concept of grace. Grace is the free and unmerited gift of God; it is thus something that is *given* and as such becomes the *property* of the one to whom it is given. Thus it is distinct from a favor, which is something done for someone and as such remains *external* to the beneficiary. When grace is received, it is internalized, like food or nourishment as distinct from a crutch, say, which merely aids the person with a broken ankle, but does not heal it. And the grace Mary received was that of being conceived without Original Sin. That state of sinlessness, of course, defines her very nature; and as such is better rendered by "full of grace" than by "highly favored".

Consider Mary's immediate response to the angel's salutation, "Fear not, Mary, for you have found *grace* with God" (Luke 1:30). Unsurprisingly, the Greek word rendered here as "grace" is *charis*. At this salutation it says that Mary was "troubled." Anyone, of course would be disturbed by the sort of news Mary received from Gabriel. But her response, as Luke records it, *precedes* the news that she is to bear the Messiah and *follows* the acclamation, *"Hail, full of grace, the Lord is with you: blessed are you among women."* It may be said that she was troubled by the angel himself; but it is hard to believe that there is no significance in how Luke recounts the most important event since Man's Fall from grace in the Garden. We have to wonder whether a declaration of God's favor, even by an Angel, would so trouble Mary? Later, during her visit to her cousin Elizabeth, who was soon to give birth in her old age to John the Baptist, Mary utters what Catholic Tradition calls her *Magnificat* from the first word (of the Latin text) of her formal thanksgiving to God, in which she expresses her *un*troubled delight in God's favor.

In this her exquisite prayer of gratitude, Mary is no longer troubled only grateful, although much trouble lay ahead for her as Simeon, the "just and devout" man of Jerusalem, who had prophesied to her when she and Joseph had Jesus formally presented in the Temple eight days after His birth (Luke 2:22–40)[4], to fulfill the requirements of the Law. It appears then that Mary's initial troubled response at the Annunciation was to have been at the *manner* in which Gabriel addressed her, which, upon consideration, we can see had to have disturbed her.

What, then, is the Angel, saying about Mary in his salutation, if he is not telling her simply that God has looked favorably on her? The answer lay in part in the grammatical use of the verb *cheritoō* with *kecharitōmenē*, which is the form of that verb in the perfect tense. Now the perfect tense, as any manual of grammar will tell you, indicates a completed action, the effects of which still continue in the present. What is meant then is that Mary *has already* received God's grace in some way and that she has received it in its fullness. What's more, she did not know she had received it; otherwise, the Angel's telling her would not have disturbed her. Blass and DeBrunner's *Greek Grammar of the New Testament*, a standard advanced grammar, tells us that "[i]t is permissible, on Greek grammatical and linguistic grounds, to paraphrase *kecharitōmenē* as *completely, perfectly, enduringly endowed with grace*"[5] (my emphasis).

Whatever grace Mary had received, the news of it surprised and disturbed her. Imagine that you experienced unexpectedly some kind of private revelation that left you with an unshakable certainty that you were the smartest person that had ever been or ever will be. You had never taken an IQ test, so this came as a complete surprise though you had always been regarded as a very bright girl. Secondarily, it was also revealed to you that with your genius you will produce a cure for every known disease and thus save the lives of countless millions. To be singled out in this way from every other human being would, doubtless, be disturbing at

---

4. "And Simeon blessed them and said to Mary his mother, "Behold, this child is appointed for the fall and rising of many in Israel, and for a sign that is opposed (*and a sword will pierce through your own soul also*), so that thoughts from many hearts may be revealed." (34—35).

5. Blass and DeBrunner, *Greek Grammar of the New Testament*, 166; see also 175.

first, for suddenly from that moment nothing would be the same for you.

There is something else about Gabriel's Annunciation to Mary that is worth taking into account when considering the Virgin Mary in respect of her Immaculate Conception. In his *Commentary on the Hail Mary*, St. Thomas Aquinas observes something significant about the character of the angel's salutation of Mary, namely, its *reverence*. This may not seem strange until we consider that never before, as witnessed by every instance of angelic visitations in the Old Testament, has an angel revered a human being; it has always been the other way round. The angels who, in the order of creation, are above human beings, and who directly apprehend God and act as His messengers, have always been objects of awe and reverence. But here at the Annunciation we see an angel—a very powerful one as Gabriel by tradition is known as an archangel—pays honor to a young woman. This is why in the art of the Annunciation Gabriel is so often shown to be kneeling in salutation before Mary. She is to the angelic creation someone unique among the human creation. It would perhaps be enough to suppose that her uniqueness lay entirely in that she has been chosen to bear the Son of God but for the way the angel salutes her, "Hail, full of grace!". "Full of grace", spoken by a supernatural being of unimaginable power, meant something to Mary that disturbed her natural complacency (she was completely happy in her religion, her family, her betrothed, etc.,) but which she fully accepted with complete trust in God.

Mary would not, of course, have understood the full meaning of the Angel's salutation that she was from her conception untainted by the Sin of Adam; but she knew from the strange words and the Angel's stranger behavior toward her that God had in some way singled her out from the entire race of men for a special purpose and that somehow this had, without her knowledge, always been so.

There are those, even among Catholic Christians, who wish to play down or even cast doubt on the Immaculate Conception of Mary, and insist that St. Thomas Aquinas, the premier theologian of the Roman Church, rejected the idea of the Immaculate Conception. But, while there are certainly *some* Catholic historians and theologians who hold that St. Thomas rejected the notion that the Blessed Virgin was conceived free of original sin, it is only an opinion and has no general acceptance among the *cognoscenti*. There has been much discussion over centuries whether St. Thomas did or did not deny that the Blessed Virgin was immaculately conceived, and many learned books have been written to show that he had not in fact actually concluded against it. It should also be noted that even were it true, it was the *idea* of an immaculate conception and not the Church's *doctrine* that St. Thomas would have rejected; for in the 13th century the Immaculate Conception had not yet been declared a dogma of the Church and so no one was as yet *obliged* to accept it as such though a great many already believed it to be true.

Admittedly, that so great a theologian to have rejected the idea could be considered grounds for doubting the doctrine. But we may be certain that even if St. Thomas did not accept the idea of the immaculate conception of the Blessed Virgin, neither did he ever teach anything to the contrary. His objections were merely speculatory, not a declaratory judgement. His explicit teaching with regard to Mary's purity as the human means of the Incarnation is however unmistakable: "Purity is constituted by a recession from impurity, and therefore it is possible to find some creature purer than all the rest, namely one not contaminated by any taint of sin; such was the purity of the Blessed Virgin, who was immune from original and actual sin, yet under God, inasmuch as there was in her the potentiality of sin"[6]. While he did teach that Mary too, like all men, required redemption, having "the potentiality of sin", the Church has always affirmed that truth and reaffirms it in her dogmatic definition of the Immaculate Conception: "the Blessed Virgin Mary, from the first moment of her conception, by a singular grace and privilege of almighty God, and *in view of the merits of Jesus Christ, Savior of the human race*"[7] (my emphasis) The text of

---

6. Aquinas, *Commentary on the Book of Sentences*, 1, d. 44, q. 1, a. 3, ad 3.
7. Pius IX, *Ineffabilis*.

the dogmatic definition does not expressly declare that Mary was redeemed, but Pius IX in the same Bull, *Ineffabilis* (1854), in which he defines the dogma, states that "she was redeemed in the most sublime way". The extraordinary truth of the matter is that Christ was the redeemer of His Mother and carried out His redemptive action in her "in the most perfect way"[8] from the first moment of her existence. The Second Vatican Council proclaimed that the Church "admires and exalts in Mary *the most excellent fruit of* the Redemption" (my emphasis)[9]. So, the fact is that St. Thomas never conclusively affirmed or denied the idea of Mary having ben immaculately conceived, as the Church eventually formulated it in her dogmatic definition and I would not presume even to attempt to settle what is an abstruse controversy among professional theologians. For the plain person considering the question it is enough to know that, far from being at odds with the dogma, it was St. Thomas's theological work that provided the basis for the Church's final definition of it.

---

8. Pius XII, *Fulgens corona*.
9. *Sacrosanctum Concilium*, 103.

4

Mary and the Life of Jesus

MARY'S PURITY, HER BEING free of original sin, prepared her not only to bear the God-Man, but also to raise Him. As Jesus was fully human as well as fully divine, He, as would any human child, required to be reared and educated. His perfection only made that a much less complicated and disappointing task. In fact, it made it for Mary and Joseph an infinitely rewarding task. To have raised Jesus was to have learned from Him. For Joseph, who was not free of original sin, it was purifying. But for Mary, it was a journey that brought her ever closer to God, deepening her already potent intimacy. In a real sense then, in raising the Son of God, she was being, in a real sense, raised *by* Him into an ever-greater knowledge of God and into an ever-greater intimacy with Him. Raising Jesus brought her, in a word, ever closer to God. Mary was thus in a unique relationship to Jesus which transcended that of mother and son, being rather the relation of soul (mind, heart, and will) to God. While Jesus remained in the world, their relationship, in this spiritual sense, was unique. But it would not remain so. When His work of Redemption was finished, this relationship with God in Christ which Mary enjoyed became possible for all men and women. Mary's relationship to Jesus *as* the Redeemer would become the paradigm for every Christian. Her relationship in this important sense (although in another sense she would always remain unique) could not remain unique, because what God did for Mary at conception in preventing her inheriting original sin was to make her completely pure, and to do this in every soul was the whole purpose of His coming into the world. It was in view of His finished work that Jesus declared, when it was said to Him, "Blessed is the womb that bore thee, and the breasts that suckled thee", "rather', He said, 'blessed are they who hear the word of God, and keep it" (Luke 11: 27-8). Mary's relation to Him was of creature to Creator, of redeemed to Redeemer, servant to Lord and Master, and (eventually), in some true sense, a relation of friends, of two persons with a common purpose. In raising Jesus, Mary became more and more a willing and knowing participant in His work of salvation. She continually learned of Him and cooperated with Him as her Lord even as He did with her as His mother while He was still growing up and under her authority.

Naturally, Mary's knowledge and cooperation developed as Jesus' knowledge of Himself and divine purpose developed during the years in which He grew toward His maturity. They were two unique people in the world with a common, unique purpose: He to fulfill His act of Redemption and she to help Him accomplish it. Of course, it is only by His leave that she helps Him, for she does nothing He does not ask her to do. At first, there was much she didn't and couldn't understand, but which would become clearer to her later in her Son's adult life as she followed Him with the others listening to Him from afar and pondering His words. It is not too much to suppose that Jesus and Mary had by this stage in their relationship become genuine friends as they shared a common purpose. Though now she followed *Him* and subjected her will to *His* as He was no longer a child under her authority. He would have doubtless explained Himself and His great purpose to her as He himself entered more fully into the knowledge of His divine nature and purpose. For Mary was always to be a part of His work even once He had established His Kingdom and she had followed Him in death into the life prepared for her from all eternity. And she of course had many questions to ask Him as she had for so many years "pondered these things in her heart" all that she had heard and experienced from the time the angel announced His birth; her cousin Elizabeth's prophecy when Mary visited her; the miraculous Birth and the adoration of the Magi; Simeon's prophecy in the Temple, and Jesus' unexpected words to her when they found Him in the Temple in Jerusalem after losing Him for three days. Mary must have thought a good deal as well about what she had heard read from the Scriptures about her Son, the Messiah.

While Jesus was still a child, Mary's task (and Joseph's while he lived) was the natural one of raising a boy to manhood. A mother's natural experience of faithfully raising her child, the many years of teaching, sharing, suffering, celebrating, loving, creates a very deep bond between mother and child as most mothers know. At the natural level, Mary's experience was no different than any other mother of a happy child. But because Jesus, Who, we do well to remember, had two natures and thus was fully God as well as being fully human, Mary's natural relation to Him was necessarily experienced at a higher, supernatural level, and, therefore was far deeper and more intense (not necessarily or simply emotionally) than any natural mother's experience. Mary was experiencing in a real and intense way a perfect communion with her Lord and God that every faithful Christian seeks and, though imperfectly because of sin, experiences. Mary was, in a very real way, the first Christian, in that she enjoyed an intimate relationship with Jesus Christ as her Lord, and to Whom her entire being, heart, mind, and soul, was devoted. She was the first Christian because she was the first to be redeemed and to devote herself to Him. God had sanctified her at the moment of her conception, and hence, she forever and completely belonged to God to do His will—the "Handmaid of the Lord"—and so would devote herself likewise to His Son. She too was, like her divine Son, the "Servant of the Lord", as He was known to the Prophets.

5

Mary's Visitation to Elizabeth

MARY LONG AND QUIETLY meditated on the memories of her most poignant experiences with her divine Son, from the Annunciation to the Wedding at Cana, when He left her household to make Himself known to the world. They were (as we shall see) graces given her as revelations or epiphanies of God's great purpose which she gradually came to understand. The first, besides the Annunciation itself, which we've already considered, is the Visitation, Mary's visit to her cousin Elizabeth, who was soon to give birth to John the Baptist. The Church has recognized this as a significant event for the same reason St. Luke was inspired to record it (Luke 1:39-56). It is one of very few instances in the Scriptures in which Mary's own words are recorded. Here, it is her Magnificat as quoted above. We have to suppose these events were recorded at all because they were the events which Mary herself considered to be most significant for only she could have related them, directly or indirectly, to Luke and especially to John the Apostle, with whom she lived for some years[1].

Mary was told at the Annunciation that her cousin, Elizabeth, was also with child and in three months would give birth. This was a clear sign to Mary that this other birth was somehow also of

1. See John 19: 26-7.

25

God, not only because the angel should have announced it to her in conjunction with the news of her bearing the Messiah, but because she knew her cousin was too old to bear a child unless it too was in some way part of God's great purpose. Mary set out almost immediately for the hill country of Judea where Elizabeth lived with her husband, Zechariah. It was a long and difficult journey of many miles by donkey through rugged hill country; and for a poor girl, who was also pregnant there were no amenities only dangers, although she had, very likely, the comfort and protection of Joseph as well as, we may suppose, an invisible company of angels. Any number of very reasonable fears and apprehensions must have occurred to her, but she was the Lord's servant and understood His will to be that she was to go to her cousin. Mary could have had no clear understanding why she should go to Elizabeth, except that her cousin needed her. That would have been sufficient reason for Mary in any circumstances, but still more now that she perceived that she and Elizabeth were related now by more than blood.

Mary's going to Elizabeth is a remarkable act of mercy. The angel did not inform Mary in vain of the extraordinary fact of her cousin's pregnancy. God's messages are never pointless. Neither are they ever wasted when addressed to a pure heart, recollected and totally surrendered to His will. And yet the angel told Mary no more than her cousin's condition; she was not *commanded* to go to Elizabeth. She didn't need to be. Mary's disposition to love made her always ready at the mere suggestion. It is worth noting here that Mary didn't hesitate and St. Luke himself makes special note that she went "with haste", almost impulsively. Mary doesn't consider her own delicate condition or the trouble she will be put to by the journey. Neither does she let her natural inclination to solitude and silence and contemplation—she is the kind of person who is naturally disposed to these things—persuade her otherwise. We might suppose anyone else in her position to have excused herself from the arduous and dangerous journey by reason of her vocation: she was chosen to bear the Son of God and surely it is natural and proper that she take no unnecessary risks, and that so high a calling would exempt her from the ordinary duties of life.

No, Mary, who is not a servant of her nature or to an idea of her grandeur, acts generously, cheerfully, even impetuously, to place herself at the service of her cousin. This is not mere natural affection, but natural affection operating under the inspiration of the Holy Spirit, for her soul was a pure receptacle of God's grace. It was the Love of God, which she was literally carrying in her womb, that inspired her natural feelings for a dear family relation. So much of what I've described of Mary's act is, of course, not in the biblical text; but have you ever known someone act from charity with a full heart? (It is to be hoped we have all had such exemplars in life.) There is nothing calculated about such acts; they are all generosity and cheerfulness. St. Paul tells us that charity burns (2Cor. 5:14) and it burned unhindered in Mary's untainted heart of mercy.

What happens when Mary arrives should make us think and wonder. Mary's act of mercy in coming to help her cousin in need precipitates another act of God's mercy to Elizabeth and to the child in her womb, something which Mary could not have anticipated or effected by her own doing. We are told that when Elizabeth heard Mary's greeting, "the baby leapt in her womb, and Elizabeth was filled with the Holy Spirit". A small detail here worth noting about Mary's humility: despite being keenly aware of the supreme honor given her of bearing the Son of the Most High, Mary, we may suppose, deliberately and self-effacingly greets Elizabeth first, observing the ordinary social and familial deference due to an elder in the social hierarchy of that time and culture. Just as in her coming to her cousin aid in the first place, Mary's humility is completely unaffected by the knowledge of her unique status. Elizabeth then cries out a blessing on Mary and on the Infant in Mary's womb. And in response, Mary proclaims her "Magnificat," her psalm of praise to God for choosing His poor handmaid to be the vessel from which He will accomplish the great outpouring of His Mercy upon Israel and the world as He promised. What happens to Elizabeth and to the child inside her is infinitely more than the natural joy felt when welcoming a dear relation or the usual movement of a baby still *in utero*. Mary brings to her cousin Something infinitely more valuable than her assistance in a difficult time; she brings hidden within her God's real, physical presence. Catholic Tradition teaches (not dogmatically) that at this moment John the Baptist was cleansed of original sin. Is this belief unfounded? Consider the angel's prophecy to Zachariah concerning John the Baptist which Luke records in the first chapter of his gospel:

> But the angel said to him, 'Do not be afraid, Zechariah, for your prayer is heard, and your wife Elizabeth will bear you a son, and you shall call his name John. And you will have joy and gladness, and many will rejoice at his birth; for he will be great before the Lord, and he shall drink no wine nor strong drink, *and he will be filled with the Holy Spirit, even from his mother's womb.*[italics mine] And he will turn many of the sons of Israel to the Lord their God, and he will go before him in the spirit and power of Elijah, to turn the hearts of the fathers to the children, and the disobedient to the wisdom of the just, to make ready for the Lord a people prepared'. (Lk. 1:13 *ff*)

The Baptist's leaping "for joy" in Elizabeth's womb signifies, according to the earliest Church Fathers, that he was at that moment freed from original sin[2] and that he never sinned personally throughout the course of his short but immensely important life[3]. The Catholic Church does not teach this as a belief necessary for salvation. But if we consider John's miraculous conception in the barren womb of an old woman, and God's purpose for bringing him into the world as the final prophet, the Precursor, to prepare the way for His own advent into the world to usher in a New

---

2. This is to be distinguished from Mary's immaculate *conception*. John the Baptist was *cleansed* of Original Sin, Mary never had it.

3. St. Augustine, when commenting on the propriety of the Church's celebration of the birthday of the Baptist as well his day of martyrdom, explained that its propriety was due to the Baptist having come into the world without sin. See Sermon 293, 1-3 in *PL* 38, 1397-1398.
   The teaching is based on Luke's account of the angel's promise to Zachariah: "the angel said to him: Fear not, Zachary, for thy prayer is heard; and they wife Elizabeth shall bear thee a son, and thou shalt call his name John: and thou shalt have joy and gladness, and many shall rejoice in his nativity. For he shall be great before the Lord; and shall drink no wine nor strong drink: and he shall be filled with the Holy Ghost, even from his mother's womb" (8-17).

Covenant and renew mankind through a New Adam and a New Eve[4], considering it, no one need find it difficult to believe that God would render His greatest of all prophets (Matt. 11,11), freed of the burden of sin. It should be noted here that what happened to John the Baptist is not the same as Mary's immaculate conception; for John was conceived in Original Sin but was then *cleansed* of it before his birth .

However we understand the Baptist's being "filled with the Holy Spirit" in the womb, the most significant thing here for our purpose is that God made this happen through Mary, God's servant, who brought His physical Presence to Elizabeth and to John, carrying Him in her womb, and thus mediating to another human being His life-giving and salvific power. We should be astonished by this, for it is astonishing that the Holy Spirit should sanctify the infant John through Mary at this meeting. But it is astonishing not as a mere story, but as a true example of the power of God. Mary, who bears Jesus the Savior in her womb, does nothing more than cooperate with the Love that was in her by an act of mercy to another mother-to-be, who bears within her the Savior's precursor to prepare the way for His divine work. God does the rest. John, the Precursor, is thus especially prepared for his unique role as the last prophet to prepare the way for the Messiah. And even his mother receives an extraordinary blessing, she is "filled with the Holy Spirit", which moves her to declare prophetically to and about Mary something no less extraordinary: "Blessed are you among women, and blessed is the fruit of your womb! And why is this granted me, *that the mother of my Lord should come to me?* [italics mine] For behold, when the voice of your greeting came to my ears, the babe in my womb leaped for joy. And blessed is she who believed that there would be a fulfillment of what was spoken to her from the Lord" (Lk 1: 42—45).

This is obviously a prophetic utterance inspired by the Holy Spirit. Elizabeth could not have known of Mary's condition (she would not yet be "showing" as we say) nor of the angel's revelation

---

4. See Irenaeus, *Against Heresies*, Bk V, 19-20 for an early theological explication of Christ as the New Adam and Mary as the New Eve.

to her. More astonishing, she calls Mary "the mother of my Lord". Elizabeth doesn't know what has just occurred to the child in her own womb except that it leapt in her when Mary greeted her[5], only that the fruit of Mary's womb is "blessed", He Who is the Lord.

To this Mary, in her true blessedness, responds with her Magnificat, her exquisite psalm of praise and gratitude to God:

> My soul proclaims the greatness of the Lord,
> my spirit rejoices in God my Savior
> for he has looked with favor on his lowly servant.
> From this day all generations will call me blessed:
> the Almighty has done great things for me,
> and holy is his Name.
>
> He has mercy on those who fear him
> in every generation.
> He has shown the strength of his arm,
> he has scattered the proud in their conceit.
>
> He has cast down the mighty from their thrones,
> and has lifted up the lowly.
> He has filled the hungry with good things,
> and the rich he has sent away empty.
>
> He has come to the help of his servant Israel
> for he remembered his promise of mercy,
> the promise he made to our fathers,
> to Abraham and his children forever. [6]

---

5. John's prophetic consecration in the womb of Elizabeth has a precedent in the Old Testament in the prophetic consecration of Jeremiah while still in his mother's womb: "Before I formed you in the womb I knew you; and before you came forth out of the womb I sanctified you, and I ordained you a prophet unto the nations" (Jer. 1,5).

6. Magnificat *anima mea Dominum; Et exultavit spiritus meus in Deo salutari meo, Quia respexit humilitatem ancillae suae; ecce enim ex hoc beatam me dicent omnes generationes. Quia fecit mihi magna qui potens est, et sanctum nomen ejus, Et misericordia ejus a progenie in progenies timentibus eum. Fecit potentiam brachio suo; Dispersit superbos mente cordis sui. Deposuit potentes de sede, et exaltavit humiles. Esurientes implevit bonis, et divites dimisit inanes.*

Having been proclaimed "blessed among women", Mary in her profound humility acclaims God as the Author of all her blessings and of all blessings. In her immense joy in God's goodness and mercy, Mary entirely forgets herself except as the recipient of them. "From this day all generations will call me blessed" will doubtless strike most modern ears as somewhat conceited. But to proclaim such about herself without any embarrassment or self-consciousness, as it is the simple truth—for she says nothing that God has not already told her, is the essence of humility. Conscious of the tremendous honor done her and even of the honor paid her by her cousin and—let's not forget—by the angel, Mary is yet deeply mindful of her "lowliness" as a mere creature and servant of God. She assumes no credit for anything. She understands her essential nothingness before the One Who gave her everything even her existence. Mary knows in acknowledgment of Him Who is Uncreated Being that she is nothing in and of herself. And yet she is above all creatures to be honored, not because she could have accomplished anything of what we honor her for, but because through her God has given us the gift of Himself. When we honor Mary, we do not exalt Man but God.

Sucepit Israel, puerum suum, recordatus misericordiae suae, Sicut locutus est ad patres nostros, Abraham et semeni ejus in saecula.

6

Mary as the Ark of the New Covenant

IT IS BECAUSE MARY is the preeminent vessel or agent of God's mercy through Jesus Christ to His creatures that the Church has always regarded her as the "Ark of the New Covenant", prefigured in the Ark of the Covenant of the Old Testament[1]. This, doubtless, strikes the Protestant as pretty outlandish, but one can see in Scripture a clear parallel between Mary and the Ark of the Covenant as the parallel we have seen between Eve, our first Mother through whose disobedience (and primarily Adam's) sin came into the world, and Mary, the Mother of Grace through whose obedience came our Salvation in Christ.

The Ark of the Covenant, as told in the 25th chapter of the Book of Exodus, was built by Moses at God's command and to very exacting specifications and contained the Tablets of the Law, a golden jar holding the manna, and Aaron's rod (Heb. 9:4). To house the Ark a tabernacle was built, also at God's command and to His exact specifications. It was, by design, a tent and, thus, a movable sanctuary to hold the sign of God's Presence to be always visible

---

1. Cf. an excellent explication of this at www.catholic.com/magazine/articles/mary-the-ark-of-the-new-covenant, which I closely follow here.

to the people of Israel throughout their pilgrimage to the Promised Land. When the Ark and Tabernacle were completed, God filled the Tabernacle with His glory as a cloud: "The cloud (Heb. *schekinah*) covered the tabernacle of the testimony, and the glory of the Lord filled it" (Ex 40:34-35; see also Nm. 9:18, 22). The verb "to cover" in Hebrew means "to overshadow" as a canopy.[2] This overshadowing of the divine Presence and the cloud metaphor are not uncommon in the theophanies found throughout Scripture when God reveals His Presence whether obscurely or luminously: Moses on Mount Sinai, the Tabernacle, the Pillar of Cloud guiding the Hebrews as they wandered in the desert, with Solomon at the dedication of the temple, on the mountain of Transfiguration when the Spirit in the "cloud came and overshadowed" Jesus, Moses, and Elijah and "a voice came out of the cloud, saying, 'This is my Son, my Chosen; listen to him!'"; and, finally, at the Ascension when a cloud that took Jesus out of sight and the "cloud" that the angel said will reveal Him at His final coming[3]. The language used is the same when the Spirit of God comes upon the Virgin Mary and "overshadows" her (like a cloud), in order that she conceive the Son of God.

Like so much in the religion of the Israelites in the Old Testament, the Ark of the Covenant was meant to signify and thus anticipate what would in and through Christ be fulfilled in the New Testament, viz., the Divine Presence, by His Incarnation and by extension, as the Catholic Church teaches, in the Holy Eucharist. So, what the Ark of the Covenant only signified, was through Mary made a reality. She becomes an effective sign of God's presence as she was to Elizabeth, who acclaimed her "blessed among women" and even to the yet unborn John the Baptist, who leapt for joy at His presence as Mary approached[4].

It would have astonished a first-century Jew (though perhaps better understood symbolically) as much as it does any modern

---

2. See '*skk*' in Botterweck, *A Theological Dictionary of the Old Testament*.

3. See *The Catechism of the Catholic Church*, §697.

4. Mary's coming to Elizabeth is a sourcce of blessing, just as was the coming of the ark for the house of Obededom. See 2 Sam 6:11.

Protestant that Mary is revealed as the Ark of the New Covenant to the Apostle John in his vision while exiled on the Isle of Patmos. In Chapter 11 of his Revelation John writes, "Then God's temple in heaven was opened, and the ark of his covenant was seen within his temple." (v. 19). Note what *immediately* follows his vision of the Ark: "And a great portent appeared in heaven, a woman clothed with the sun, with the moon under her feet, on her head a crown of twelve stars; she was with child" (12,1-2). This juxtaposition of what may seem separate visions at the end of chapter 11 and the beginning of 12, is more astonishing when we consider that the ancient manuscripts of the Scriptures have no chapter divisions, which were an innovation of the 12th Century. So far as his narrative indicates, writing as he did continuously without chapter breaks, John's seeing the ark and the woman clothed with the sun might very well have been aspects of the same object envisioned, not different objects. That is to say, the Woman Clothed with the Sun was *meant* to be associated with the Ark of the Covenant as aspects of the Blessed Virgin Mother of God. Now, by the time of John's writing, it was already widely believed among Christians that Mary had been assumed body and soul into heaven[5] So, John himself would have understood the juxtaposition of these two elements of his vision, and especially the Woman Clothed with the Sun as Mary herself, with whom the woman of John's vision has been identified since antiquity. Of course, the rich, multivalent

---

5. Soon after the building of the Church of the Holy Sepulchre in 336, the memory of the death of Christ's mother was honored by the Christians in Jerusalem on the hill close to Mt. Zion at the "Tomb of Mary," and near where the early Christian community had lived. On the hill itself was the "Place of Dormition," the place where Mary had died or "fallen asleep," and it was in the "Tomb of Mary" that she was buried.

It was as early as the early 4th century that the "Memory of Mary" was being celebrated and which a little later become the feast of the Assumption, the oldest Marian feast day in the Christian calendar. The "Memory of Mary", originally local to Palestine, was extended by the emperor to all the churches of the East. The ancient celebration of Mary's death soon was changed from the celebration of the *Dormitio* ("Falling Asleep") of the Mother of God to the "Assumption of Mary," because the feast proclaimed more than her dying; it also proclaimed that she had been taken up, body and soul, into heaven, a belief that dates back to the time of the Apostles

symbolism of John's Revelations allows for the woman to represent more than Mary alone. She has been understood to represent both the Church and Israel as well. But they are all of a piece, magnificent facets of God's work of Redemption that began with Adam, Eve, the Serpent, and the Fall and ends with Christ, the New Man, Mary, the New Eve, and, again, the Enemy now defeated in the final triumph of God's redemptive love. Of the interpretation of this passage in Revelation which regards the Woman as a symbol of the Church, Blessed John Henry Newman wrote:

> I do not deny of course that under the image of the Woman, the Church is signified; but what I would maintain is this, that the Holy Apostle would not have spoken of the Church under this particular image unless there had existed a Blessed Virgin Mary who was exalted on high and the object of veneration of all the faithful.
>
> No one doubts that the "man child" spoken of is an allusion to Our Lord: why then is not the "Woman" an allusion to His Mother? This surely is the obvious sense of the words; of course they have a further sense also, which is the scope of the image; doubtless the Child represents the children of the Church, and doubtless the Woman represents the Church; this, I grant, is the real or direct sense, but what is the sense of the symbol under which that real sense is conveyed? I answer, they are not personifications but Persons. This is true of the Child, therefore it is true of the Woman.
>
> But again: not only Mother and Child, but a serpent is introduced into the vision. Such a meeting of man, woman and serpent has not been found in Scripture since the beginning of Scripture, and now it is found in its end. Moreover, in the passage in the Apocalypse, as if to supply, before Scripture came to an end, what was wanting in its beginning, we are told, and for the first time, that the serpent in Paradise was the evil spirit. If the dragon of St. John is the same as the serpent of Genesis, and the man-child is "the seed of the woman," why is not the woman herself she whose seed the man-child

is? And, if the first woman is not an allegory, why is the second? If the first woman is Eve, why is not the second Mary?[6]

Newman's understanding of Mary came not from medieval Catholic sources, as some might suppose, but from the teaching of the Fathers. When E.B. Pusey, a leader with Newman of the Oxford Movement, denounced the Catholic devotion to the Blessed Virgin as exaggerated and a chief obstacle to Church unity[7], Newman responded[8] by demonstrating in his masterly way that the doctrine of the Blessed Virgin held by the Early Fathers is in all important respects the same as that held by Catholics of his own day. He goes on to say that it was the Fathers who made a Catholic of him—an avowal made by many a modern convert from the Protestant tradition.

Another consideration of Mary as the Ark of the New Covenant in light of this passage in Luke's Gospel is David's visit to the Ark of the Covenant as related in II Samuel 6 (II Kings in some Bibles). If we compare closely the two accounts, we can see that Luke has rendered his narrative in such a way as to parallel the Scriptural narrative as he found it in the second Book of Kings[9]:

---

6. Newman, *Difficulties Felt by Anglicans in Catholic Teaching*, 54 -70 .
7. See Pusey, *An Eirenicon*.
8. Newman, *Letter to Pusey*.
9. This parallel comparison is taken from www.Catholic Answers.com/magazine/articles/Mary-the-ark-of-the-new-covenant.

The ark traveled to the house of Obed-edom in the hill country of Judea (2 Sam. 6:1-11).	Mary traveled to the house of Elizabeth and Zechariah in the hill country of Judea (Luke 1:39).
Dressed as a priest, David danced and leapt in front of the ark (2 Sam. 6:14).	John the Baptist—of priestly lineage—leapt in his mother's womb at the approach of Mary (Luke 1:41).
David asks, "How can the ark of the Lord come to me?" (2 Sam. 6:9).	Elizabeth asks, "Why is this granted me, that the mother of my Lord should come to me?" (Luke 1:43).
David shouts in the presence of the ark (2 Sam. 6:15).	Elizabeth "exclaimed with a loud cry" in the presence of the Mary (Luke 1:42).
The ark remained in the house of Obed-edom for three months (2 Sam. 6:11).	Mary remained in the house of Elizabeth for three months (Luke 1:56).
The house of Obed-edom was blessed by the presence of the ark (2 Sam. 6:11).	The word *blessed* is used three times; surely the house was blessed by God (Luke 1:39-45).
The ark returns to its home and ends up in Jerusalem, where God's presence and glory is revealed in the temple (2 Sam. 6:12; 1 Kgs. 8:9-11).	Mary returns home and eventually ends up in Jerusalem, where she presents God incarnate in the temple (Luke 1:56; 2:21-22).

The parallel between these narratives is far too close to be coincidental. It is reasonable to suppose that Luke is at pains to present to his readers, who (the Jews at least) would not have missed the parallelism he is drawing, to present Mary as the Ark of the New Covenant in Christ. The parallelism is still more obvious when we consider as well the contents of the old Ark. Inside the Ark of the Old Covenant were the stone tablets of the Law, on which were inscribed God's word; inside Mary was the living Word of God incarnate. Then there was the urn filled with manna, miraculous bread God sent from heaven to feed the His people in the wilderness; Mary's womb held the Bread of Life (Jn. 6:35-41) come down from heaven. Also in the old Ark was the rod of Aaron that budded demonstrating his authenticity as the true High Priest; Mary carries within her the Eternal High Priest—Jesus, Who was "made a high priest forever according to the order of Melchisedech." (Heb. 6:20)

So, it seems pretty clear that the woman clothed with the sun whom John sees in his vision in Revelation can very reasonably be understood to be the Blessed Virgin clothed with the Glory of God, resplendent as the old Ark of the Covenant was in its proper cloud of glory, and thus is she revealed as the Ark of the New Covenant who delivers to the world the One Whom the Enemy would destroy, but Who will rule the world at last with an all-consuming justice. It should not go unnoticed that the "Woman clothed with the sun" is crowned, but does not rule. She is crowned because she is the mother of the King. Nor should it be missed that she is only *clothed* with the sun but it is the moon she has under foot. Mary's glory is necessarily derivative as the moon's light is only a reflection of the sun's, as St. John's vision indicates. Mary's glory is unequalled among mortals, but it is God's own glory reflected in His lowly handmaiden.

7

Mary and the Birth of Jesus

FOR NINE MONTHS JESUS was present primarily with Mary alone in her body. Any mother who wants the birth of the child she carries and awaits it expectantly knows the natural bonding that occurs between her and her child. Mary, of course, experienced this natural bonding too, but because the Child with Whom she was bonding was God Himself, Who was uniquely present to her, not merely physically. Mary's bonding with Jesus had at once a natural and mystical or supernatural quality, because her soul was free of the encumbrances of original sin, and by virtue of the mystery of the Incarnation. Jesus was a completely *human* Being; and thus His presence in Mary's womb was spiritual as well as biological. Mary's soul, her heart, the very seat or core of her being and personhood bonded with Her Lord, experiencing in her heart in a profoundly contemplative way the mystery of God's Presence in her for the nine months she carried Him. The Christian who is deeply united to God in charity (*agape*) and prayer and thus free from any attachment to or habitual inclination to sin—alas, all too few of us—can begin to understand her experience.

When a child is born, the bonding, as we all know, intensifies. And when Jesus is born, Mary enters a new phase of her unique relationship with Him. The Incarnate God now gives Himself to his mother as a tiny baby, helpless and utterly dependent on her, expecting from her all that she can give Him in this the beginning of His earthly life. Reciprocally, Mary must give herself wholly to Him as His natural mother. The waiting and the relative docility of the pregnancy is over. She has now to do all the things a mother needs to do to ensure the health and safety and contentment of her child. Her love as God's handmaiden is now less passive and contemplative and more active, even busy. It is at one level all very natural, but because it is—*mirabile dictu!*—God Himself she is caring for, all her activity binds her ever more closely to the One Who has united her to Himself in this unique way.

While Jesus remained in her womb, He was still completely hidden from the world, but with His birth, He is revealed first to Mary and to Joseph and then to the world. He becomes her complete joy which she shares with the world. *He was in the world, and the world was made by him, and the world knew Him not. He came unto his own, and his own received Him not. But as many as received him, He gave them power to be made the sons of God, to them that believe in His name. Who are born, not of blood, nor of the will of the flesh, nor of the will of man, but of God. And the Word was made flesh, and dwelt among us, and we saw His glory, the glory as it were of the only begotten of the Father, full of grace and truth.* (Jn. 1, 10-14). Mary was the first to receive Him and to witness His glory and to be thus united to Him. This union, as I said, was at once physical and biological and mystical, by which her soul, pure and untainted, received by grace the One Who would one day take her to be with Him and share with Him the glory of His Father, as He promised to "all who believe". One of the prayers of the Angelus, the old and venerable Catholic devotion commemorating the Incarnation, says:

> Pour forth, we beseech Thee, O Lord, Thy grace into our hearts; that we, to whom the incarnation of Christ, Thy Son, was made known by the message of an angel, may by His Passion and Cross be brought to the glory of His Resurrection, through the same Christ Our Lord.

The prayer identifies the Christian praying it with the Blessed Virgin in so far as she "to whom the incarnation of Christ . . . was made known by the message of an angel" preceded us in God's grace by "His Passion and Cross" to the "glory of His Resurrection". Mary, as the New Eve, is the first to enter into the glory of God; Jesus in His divine nature, of course, never left it. This prayer reminds those who pray it, as does so much else in the Catholic Marian devotions, that she, for all the honor and veneration the Church bestows upon her as "Queen of Heaven" and "Mediatrix of all the Graces", is nevertheless *one of us* who has entered into her reward. Her magnificence is not the invention of men, but the gift of God in Christ.

It cannot be emphasized too much that Mary, as the nurturing mother of Our Lord, enters into this role not merely naturally but, as she is full of the grace of God, enters it also in that mystical dimension I spoke of by the guidance of the Holy Spirit. Because her motherhood is also supernatural, it is an act of divine grace operating in and through her, even as she nestled the Divine Child to her breast and fed Him and bathed Him. As Mary gave her divine Son all that was physically in her to give, she was also giving Him her heart and mind in a mystical communion with the One Who gives her life and existence and, yes, the One Who redeemed her.

Now, at this dawn of the New Testament, the Old having come to an end with the Advent of Christ, there is much, of course, that Mary could not understand in any sort of merely rational way. No, Mary's ever deepening understanding of her Divine Son is inspired by the Holy Spirit, by Whom the Child was conceived in her and Who never leaves her but nurtures her as she nurtures the Him Who is "God with us." Mary, we may say, was absorbed in her Son. Every moment of her life in this world was in some way devoted to Him. Some might be inclined to feel sorry for Joseph. But Mary's all-consuming love for her Son was the Love *of* her Son, the special gift to her from Him Who is Love Himself; it was not natural maternal affection that excludes from moment to moment every other object, but divine love that necessarily includes all other loves, subsuming them and thus attending perfectly to every object of those loves. The love of God in Mary subsumed her love for Joseph, allowing her to respond perfectly to his needs and to his love of her and her Son as she had done so readily for her cousin, Elizabeth, when she needed her.

There is, perhaps, a tendency in recognizing the perfection of the Holy Family of Jesus, Mary, and Joseph to idealize their *circumstances*, to imagine them living without suffering or hardship or "stress", as we now call our commonplace and quotidian struggles. Certainly, much of the religious art that depicts them suggests this kind of perfect tranquility. And it is justified in so far as the art's intention is to represent the *inner* tranquility of the Holy Family. But we know that the Holy Family was poor, and though Joseph was a skilled and productive carpenter, and as such a responsible provider, we know too that there is no real poverty without suffering. But the Scriptures and even Catholic Tradition are largely silent about these years of Jesus' family life. These silent years bespeak the silence of Mary herself, her continuous contemplation of and service to her Divine Son, waiting in her silence and poverty upon God to fulfill His promise of salvation, living in most respects a very ordinary life.

8

The "Purification" of Mary and the Dedication of Jesus

THE PERIOD LEADING UP to Jesus' Mission, which leads to His Passion, Death, and Resurrection, is not altogether silent. Not long after His birth, Mary in keeping with the Jewish Law, went to the Temple at Jerusalem for purification (Lk. 2:22). According to the Mosaic law, a mother who has given birth to a male child was considered to be ritually unclean for seven days and was to remain thirty-three days (it was doubled for a female child) "in the blood of her purification". At the end of the forty days, the mother was to present herself at the Temple in Jerusalem, bringing with her a lamb for a burnt offering and a young pigeon or turtle dove as an offering for sin. This was every mother's ritual purification under Jewish law and Mary made herself no exception. If the mother was poor and unable to offer a lamb, she was to take two turtle doves or two pigeons; she would then be prayed over by the priest and thus she would be cleansed (Leviticus 12:2-8).[1] In addition to her ritual purification, the Law also required the mother to offer the male child to God if it be her first-born and, after presenting her son, to then "ransom" him with a certain sum of money, and then to offer more sacrifices for the occasion.[2]

1. *Catholic Encyclopedia*, "Candelmas".
2. Cf. Num 18:15.

It is a mark of Mary's profound humility that she strictly complied with all these ordinances of the Law. She knew herself to be in a most extraordinary way favored of God; she knew her Son to be, in some way she could not understand, divine, that He is the One Who was to come, the King, the Messiah, under Whose feet God would subject the whole world. What need then did He have of a ritual consecration or she for that matter of ritual cleansing since she was, she knew, still a virgin after the miraculous Birth? Mary might have supposed herself and her Son to be above the Law, for He certainly was above it Who gave it. But there was no presumption in her. Throughout her life, Mary never adverts to her status as Mother of God or the Messiah. That is an honor she does not make her own, wearing it like a great cape or studded tiara. Therefore, does the Church all the more lavish her with honors who claimed none for herself. Mary claimed only one "privilege", which was no privilege but her duty and deepest desire, to glorify God. And that she did in her chosen hiddenness and poverty. She would thus observe every requirement of the Law in keeping with her Son, Who, because He was truly above the Law, would fulfill it in a more profound way. And God confirms the justice of her obedience with the prophecy of Simeon the Just, who had waited all of his holy life for the coming of Messiah, Israel's Savior, and to whom the Holy Spirit had revealed that he would not die till he had seen the Lord's Christ (Lk 2:25-26). Simeon blesses Mary and the Child, and then to Mary he says prophetically, "Behold, this child is destined for the fall and rise of many in Israel, and to be a sign that will be contradicted—and you yourself a sword will pierce—so that the thoughts of many hearts may be revealed" (Lk. 2:34-35).

Simeon's prophecy amazed Mary as well as Joseph.[3] Her amazement may surprise us. After all, she had heard more astonishing things about the Child from an angel. But, nevertheless, Simeon's words, I suspect, struck Mary as quite unexpected. The angel had revealed to Mary that she would give birth to the Messiah, God's Anointed, Who, as promised, would deliver Israel.

---

3. Lk 2:33

The "Purification" of Mary and the Dedication of Jesus

Simeon's prophecy, however, reveals what Mary had perhaps never yet considered, that her Son would be *rejected*, that He would be a "sign of contradiction" and the (efficient) *cause* of "the *fall* and rise of many in Israel". What is more, he tells her that it is the destiny of *both she and* her Son to suffer by His rejection by Israel. This, of course, is all varyingly implicit in the Scriptures of the Old Testament, but there is no reason to suppose that Mary had perfectly understood it. She is now confronted with it at a moment when she is full of joyful hope; and though, amazed by the prophecy, we are not told that it troubled her. In her unqualified faith and humility, Mary understood (again, not by any rational surmise) that whatever God intends for Her Son, for herself, and for Israel, all that He promised would be fulfilled. Whatever ends He has in view in His infinite wisdom she will remain His lowly handmaiden.

Simeon, along with the temple, the sacrifices, etc. all belonged to the Old Testament, but Mary saw, heard, and understood them to be that through which God still spoke and confirmed His divine purpose. Mary pondered all these things in her contemplative heart and would come gradually to understand (her own Son with the Holy Spirit would teach her) how that the Christ would in Himself at once fulfill and transcend all that belonged to the Old Testament.

Mary's presentation of Jesus in the temple at Jerusalem was indeed a faithful adherence to the Old Testament, but it was also, whether or not Mary at that point realized it, a looking forward to the New Testament. By His consecration under the old Law, Mary through the priest formally offers Jesus to God. This Offering by the priest, Simeon, is in fact the final, culminating act of the Levitical Priesthood. After this, in effect, it ceases to be. It's *raison d'etre* has been its symbolic anticipation of the One Who would be both High Priest and Offering and Who alone could take away sins as St. Paul painstakingly explained in his Letter to the Hebrews. At this moment of Mary's offering her Son and God's in the temple, there ceases to be any reason for the old Priesthood; the Reality, the divine Priest and Sacrifice, of which the Levitical Priesthood with all its sacrifices, were only symbols, was now present among them. Simeon realizes this when he chants his praise to God (Lk. 2;29-32): "Now let Your servant go in peace; Your word has been fulfilled. My own eyes have seen the salvation which You have prepared . . ." As a man, who had all his devout life awaited the Messiah, Simeon's hymn of praise[4] concerns the expectation of everyone belonging to Israel. As a priest, his hymn concerns specifically the Levitical priesthood, for the Presentation of Jesus, the Christ, is the Old Testament priesthood's final liturgical act. It is also the beginning of a New Liturgy of a New Testament. Mary through Simeon offers her Son to God, Who eternally offers Himself to the Father in the Blessed Trinity, and Who will offer Himself in the flesh to the Father as the final Sacrifice for sins, which will be continually memorialized and re-presented (by His own command) by His Church in the Holy Eucharist until the end of time. Mary's presentation of Jesus is the beginning of a New Covenant in fulfillment of the Old made to Abraham and to his descendants (both physical and spiritual), who offered his son, Isaac, to God in obedience. And Mary is an essential part of this New Testament, willingly participating in God's redemptive plan, offering her Son back to God, Whose Son He is, and in effect to the world to be its Savior.

---

4. Catholic Tradition refers to it as the *Nunc Dimittis* after the first word in Latin that begin it.

9

Mary Loses Jesus in Jerusalem

IN CATHOLIC TRADITION AND particularly in the tradition of the specifically Marian devotion of the Holy Rosary, the finding of Jesus in the temple after being lost to Mary and Joseph for three days is classified as one of the "Joyful Mysteries" that is meditated on in praying the Rosary. Customarily then, it is Mary's joy that is considered in meditation on this event in her life. But it is not to be overlooked that Mary's joy in finding Jesus is conditioned on her anguish and sorrow in losing Him for three days. And we cannot fully understand her sorrow and anxiety unless we consider that Mary would never have forgotten the terrible slaughter of the innocents of Bethlehem eleven years earlier when Herod sought to destroy her Son. Nor can we understand the significance of Mary's unwonted separation from Jesus unless we see it as Luke (and the Holy Spirit) meant it to be understood to signify their three days separation at His Death until His Resurrection. Jesus' death and her consequent separation from Him would be the culmination of Mary's sorrows, the sword that would pierce her heart according to Simeon's prophecy. And the joy of their reunion was the joy she would have still more intensely on discovering the empty tomb and then actually seeing Him again in the Upper Room and (presumably) over those forty days before His Ascension. But their reunion did not end there; there would be the Descent of the Holy Spirit at Pentecost, when their union would deepen as she entered another stage in her ever-deepening participation in the divine Life; and finally, her unending union with Him when she would pass from this life and world into the fullness of His Kingdom.

When Joseph and Mary find Jesus, she says almost reproachfully, "Son, why have you treated us so? Your father and I have been looking anxiously for you." She doesn't conceal from Him (she would not, of course, need to) that He had worried them, but neither does she scold Him; nor can she fully express to Him the anguish of her maternal heart in His absence. She simply expresses her sadness in losing Him and her failure to understand what He was doing. What they see and hear upon finding Jesus astonishes them. He, a twelve-year-old boy, acting on his own, is seated among the learned teachers of the Temple and is amazing them by His profoundly insightful questions. Mary, walking in on this situation, could not fail to have seen and heard these men's amazement at her Son's conversation. And in that moment, she isn't able to understand what she witnesses. She has lately been all but overcome with worry; her natural, maternal heart has been wrung out. She can only ask Him why He's done this. Mary is not without need of instruction from her Lord and Jesus' answer is meant to be instructive: "How is it that you sought Me? Did you not know that I must be about My Father's business?" Jesus is, of course, not puzzled by His mother's alarm (He, doubtless, anticipated it) nor does He reproach her, for she did after all what she had to in the circumstances and she was right to do it. Even her anxiety was blameless. His question to her is, in a way, rhetorical and a gentle assertion of a simple and profound truth that she would learn well in the years to come, that before she became His mother, He was His Eternal Father's Son, and that above all else, even above her natural authority over Him as well as her natural love and concern for His physical welfare, He must do the Will of His Father, and to this all else in His life and hers is to be sacrificed. It is one of those most profound moments in Mary's life, which she carefully pondered in her heart. To this truth Mary, the pure Handmaid of the Lord, willingly, quietly, and lovingly submits, holding it in her heart in the silent contemplation that characterized her whole life. She would, in her continual submission to her Lord's will, come to understand this truth about her Son and His intentions as He pursued the Will of His Heavenly Father. Even at twelve years old, Jesus knew His mother well. As His will was one with the Father's, so His and His mother's will were united. So, he knew too that He could submit to her (and Joseph's) natural authority, as He subsequently did, without encumbering His obedience to God the Father.

This episode of losing Jesus and then finding Him in the Temple was the first recorded "coming to terms", crudely speaking, between Jesus and His mother. It was for Mary a discovery—one might almost say an epiphany—in which her divine Son revealed something more, or more clearly, of Himself to her. The next such moment would be some twenty-eight years later at the wedding at Cana just before Jesus began His public ministry in Galilee. There was no need for our Lord to labor at teaching His mother; she was the perfect student, for their hearts were one in the Holy Spirit Who possessed them both.

It is worth noting here that Mary's life was, like ours, a life of faith. She did not immediately nor perfectly understand everything that happened to her. She lived continually in the supernatural order, which in a thousand subtle ways would impress itself on her, but which she had no cognitive or rational means of sorting out or analyzing even were she so inclined as we are who struggle to trust God in the teeth of doubt and misgivings when we cannot see the sense in what He is doing. She, in the truest sense, simply trusted God and her divine Son and was faithful to them, fulfilling with an untroubled and loving confidence, all that it was given her to do and never interposing her own will, even when in the natural order, as His mother, she had a right to. We must not suppose that it was *easy* for her to raise the Son of God, though it was Mary's inexpressible joy and privilege to do so. But it was also her sorrow. For Mary, throughout her earthly life with Jesus, is preparing herself, by listening and learning in her silence and love, for His Sacrifice of Himself. She must have come to understand at some point in her growing understanding of her divine Son that He was while still in the prime of life to give Himself in death to His eternal Father for the world. Mary understood too that she must, though it pierce her heart, freely give her Son for the world even as He gives Himself.

This episode, so simple in its outlines, so profound in its significance, is for Mary (and us) a kind of epiphany of her divine Son, which, unlike previous epiphanies, He Himself initiates. It is Christ's self-revelation as the Son of *God* to (primarily) His mother who (with Joseph for a time) had still to raise Him in the world. During their time in Jerusalem, Jesus had left His parents in obedience to His eternal Father; and it was in obedience to Him that He returned to Nazareth with Mary and Joseph and "was obedient to them . . . and . . . increased in wisdom and in stature, and in favor with God and man." (Lk. 2:51-52) This episode marked a peak moment in these hidden years of our Lord's Life. Because of it (as intended), Mary and Joseph see Jesus in a different, clearer light, in which the One entrusted to their care was not merely a divinely ordained child with a great destiny, the Messiah as they understood him, but that and Someone incomparably greater.

10

Mary and the Wedding at Cana

IN THE MANY YEARS since the little "epiphany" of finding Jesus in the Temple, a highpoint in Mary's earthly life with her divine Son in which she received yet another "lesson" in His full meaning and identity in the world, Mary learned continually of our Lord through an ever-deepening love and comprehension. These years were a period of Mary's formation in divine Love under the tutelage of Love Himself; and yet they are years, we may be sure, of a quite ordinary life in the village of Nazareth. St. Luke, whose Gospel is the most comprehensively biographical, tells us nothing of what occurred in this period, because its importance lay not in its specific events but in their culmination. Comprising this period are the innumerable little things, none of them notable in themselves—cooking, cleaning, educating, etc., of a mundane life lived in obedience, simplicity, and poverty, and in the love of God. There was in this period also grief, because Joseph dies sometime in these years and Jesus loses a very loving and devout foster father, and Mary a most devout and loving husband. But Joseph's absence only concentrates Mary's attention to Jesus and is an occasion for a still deeper intimacy between them. Mary's strengthening attachment to her Son is not that of a widowed mother clinging to her only child, but of the Lord's servant and handmaid entering ever more deeply into the life of God. Thus, on the surface of things, the life of Jesus, Mary, and Joseph was plain and ordinary like ours. Beneath the surface, there surged a great rising tide of divine Love toward a culminating point.

That culminating point is when Jesus leaves His home and His mother in Nazareth to begin the work for which He came into the world and for which till now He had been preparing and being prepared. The momentous occasion of this beginning was the Wedding at Cana and His first public miracle. Mary's relationship to her Son and her whole life is about to undergo a transformation and this at many levels. For many years, Mary has been living in a profound intimacy with her Son, Who was supporting her by the craft He had learned from His father while Joseph was still alive. And although since Joseph's death Mary has had her Son all to herself, his part of their life together is about to end. At Cana, Jesus is about enter into the wide world. He is entering upon a course by which He will give Himself for the world, having first given Himself to the Father, a course that will end in His death at the hands of the powers of the world and ultimately in His overcoming the world and death in His Resurrection. Mary by now, we may suppose, has come to understand her divine Son to be the Redeemer of the world (as distinct from the Deliverer of the Jewish people) and knows that His triumph can only be accomplished by His suffering and death. So much was clear from the Prophets (especially Isaiah) and certainly if Jesus had taught his mother anything during these years of growing intimacy, certainly He had explained to her the meaning of these prophecies as He Himself came to understand them.

It will be one of Mary's distinct sorrows to relinquish her Son to His painful destiny. It is true that it was not for Mary herself to decide Jesus' movement here in beginning the Apostolic public life that would lead inexorably to His death; but it is no less true that she freely gives Him over, filled as she was with the same love that brought Him down from Heaven into the world. She does this and at Jesus' own invitation as we shall see, at the Wedding at Cana. It

Mary and the Wedding at Cana

is another of Mary's minor *fiats* which mark her willing, humble participation in God's salvation of man.

Jesus' Apostolic ministry formally was inaugurated with His Baptism, when He is publicly revealed as the Son of God: the Holy Spirit descends upon Him and the Voice of God the Father declares, "This is My Beloved Son in Whom I am well pleased". But it is at Cana, at a wedding of (presumably) one of His mother's relations, that Jesus informally and *effectively* begins His Apostolic work with a public miracle, His first miraculous sign manifesting His divine power.

The wedding celebration encounters a crisis when it is realized that the wine has run out. For the wine steward this meant at least a tremendous embarrassment as it would have been still more for the Host, his master; at worst, it would have meant the steward's job and the end of the festivities. Mary's tender heart goes out to the steward and to her relation and would spare them both such a disaster. She chooses to intervene and turns immediately to her Son, whose power is already known to her either by faith or experience, and simply tells Him, perhaps with a touch of alarm in her voice, "They have no more wine". Mary does not—cannot—command Her Son; her words to Him are rather a plea to miraculously remedy matters for the good people involved. She doesn't know what Jesus will do; she knows only by faith that He will certainly do the will and pleasure of His Heavenly Father.

Jesus' response to His mother is admittedly mysterious: "O Woman, what have you to do with me? My hour has not yet come." (John 2: 4). The first thing to bear in mind in trying to understand this baffling response is that Jesus is no longer subject to His Mother, no longer the docile, submissive son of her household and under her authority, and answers her accordingly. Although somewhat solemn, it would have not been considered cheeky or disrespectful for a young Hebrew of first-century Palestine to address his mother as "Woman"; after all, Jesus addresses His mother in the same way in that most tender of moments from the Cross. Yet, on the face of it, His words seem almost disdainful, certainly disrespectful of His mother and her request. As St. Augustine said of this passage, there is something hidden here.

Whatever our Lord means by His response, it is certainly not disrespectful. It is to be imagined that when Mary turns to Jesus their eyes meet and instantly there is a moment of the most intimate communication between mother and Son in which words are all but superfluous. Mary and Jesus understand each other perfectly. What He said was no mystery to *her*. His eyes, His tone of voice spoke to her and she received His (to us) strange words in the context of their long years together and with an understanding of Him and His mission that at that moment only they two possessed, a deep mutual understanding which even the men who had by now been called to Him, His Disciples, do not yet enjoy.

For us who haven't (or not yet) the privilege of Mary's intuitive understanding of our Lord, to understand this episode we must make a more deliberate, rational effort. Although baffling because addressed to His mother, the meaning of Jesus' words are plain enough. They can only mean something like: "Why do you ask me to do this thing now, when I have not yet begun My public life?" I don't think we can escape the obvious; the question is rhetorical and to anyone who may have been standing around listening it would have sounded like a mild refusal. But to Mary His response was not a simple refusal, but a conditional one. When Mary makes her plea to Jesus, she hasn't in the moment considered all the ramifications of His doing what she is asking Him to do; for she was, perhaps, thinking then only of the merely human predicament of her host. Jesus' response is to ask her to consider all that will eventuate from such a public act. Mary understands her Son to be asking her whether she is prepared for the eventualities His public life will effect, for she already apprehends what they will be and that she will suffer with Him. He is asking *her* for yet another of her *"fiats,"* but now it is not anything so reassuring as His Birth that is in view; it is His Death that will inevitably follow from His declaring Himself the Son of God. It is not her permission that He asks for but her participation. He wants His mother, to the fullest extent that she can, to share in His work of redemption. Yet Jesus

Mary and the Wedding at Cana

is no longer speaking as a son to his mother, but as the Redeemer of the world, the New Adam, to His partner in the Redemption, the New Eve, the woman uniquely chosen by God, who has wholly devoted herself to Him. Once Mary says "Yes" (her *fiat*) to His request or invitation to her, He is ready to meet her request for more wine. Mary's only response in this profound exchange between her and Jesus is to turn to the steward of the feast and say, "Do whatever He says".

The reader may have noticed the similarity that this episode of the Wedding at Cana bears to that of Finding of Jesus in the Temple. As we have noted before, Jesus is now wholly devoted to His "Father's business" and is no longer the docile mother's son. It is for Mary now to relinquish willingly the quiet, happy domestic life she knew till now. Jesus, while still a boy of twelve in the Temple at Jerusalem, gave His mother her first intimation of this eventuality. Then, Jesus had remained with her. But now He is about to leave her alone; and when He dies as a certain result of this movement into public life, as they both know He will, His abandonment of her (for a short time—Mary by faith knows this too) will be complete. Such is Mary now given to understand and to accept an altered relation to her Son, the seeds of which have long been germinating. He will be to her all that He ever was, but now He will be infinitely more. She can no longer have Him entirely to herself for He is about to give Himself (in His human nature) entirely to His Eternal Father for the world as a Sacrifice, the Lamb of God to be utterly consumed in and by the Fire of His Father's love that possesses Him. Mary, God's obedient servant, makes no resistance, no hesitation; she simply in the silence of her love and humility that shine in her eyes as she fixes them on those of her Son and Lord, agrees and tells the Steward to do whatever He tells him to do.

By this final change in their relationship Mary makes a full transformation from being primarily a mother to being a servant. Mary has, of course, always been both and does not cease now to be either. But her maternity, which had always been experienced largely in the natural order, is now to be wholly subsumed by, and thus raised to, the supernatural order; and this by her obedient act of self-giving love. Mary is entirely willing to relinquish her Son in this way, and yet this is enormously difficult, even painful, for her because of her natural maternal love for Jesus. Jesus Himself declares this new relation, soon after when they are back in Nazareth. St. Luke tells us that a crowd was pressing in all round Him "[a]nd his mother and brethren came to him; and they could not come at him for the crowd. And it was told him: Thy mother and thy brethren stand without, desiring to see thee. Who answering, said to them: My mother and my brethren are they who hear the word of God, and do it." (Lk 8: 19-21). By this Jesus declares the absolute superiority of the spiritual bond over the natural. Mary, His own mother, is not an exception to this order. Her maternity does not cease to be valuable or relevant, rather it is elevated to a higher order or, we may say, is subsumed by a higher value. This higher bond with her Son, which Mary now fully enters into, is not the relation of blood or natural affection, but of faith in God's word and faithful obedience to it.[1] And this new stage in her relation to Jesus will mean another painful separation from her Son but also a closer union with Him.

As the temporary loss of Him in Jerusalem twenty years before resulted in that painful three-day separation, so does this beginning of His public life and the assertion of His devotion to His Eternal Father result in His once again leaving her, but this time it is permanent. Mary embraces it with her renewed fiat, but now with greater understanding and faith that its permanence is only for the span of this life. Mary now looks to the life and world to come, which her Son had come down from Heaven to give to those who enter into this same relation to Him in faith and love that she has been the first of all mankind to enjoy.

Long established in the Marian theology and devotion of the Catholic tradition is the belief that our Lord will not refuse anything His mother asks of Him. Yet at Cana we see her making a request of Jesus on behalf of the wedding party and His seeming refusal. I have tried to show how Jesus' refusal can be understood as not so much a refusal as an invitation and reciprocal request to

---

1. Marie-Dominique Phillipe, O.P., *Mystery of Mary*, 171.

accept and participate in the Work of Redemption He is about irrevocably to begin. He knows her answer will be the same as she gave the angel Gabriel at His conception: "Behold, the handmaid of the Lord; be it done to me according to Thy word". Here at Cana, Mary, who by her obedience had brought the Savior into the world, again by her obedient act of self-giving, delivers Jesus to the world to be its Savior. Her *fiat* this time is spoken solely between them in the silent intimation of her eyes as she looks into her Son's and in her words to the steward, which, unbounded by mere historicity, are to all persons of all times: "Do whatever He tells you." With these words, Mary mediates between her Son, who has the power to do whatever is needed, and the people of the wedding party who face a crisis. And as this episode is significant by the inspiration of the Holy Spirit and thus transcends its merely historical significance, Mary likewise mediates Jesus' power to us by her maternal love for all who belong to her Son. This truth is, understandably, a rather big pill for many Protestants to swallow, but before Mary can ever be appreciated as anything more than a merely historic figure such as Rachel or Judith of the Old Testament, we must realize that she, like us, is immortal and is right now fully enjoying the vision and life of God. As I write, she is living with Christ in the fullness of the Beatific Vision and has never ceased to be the Mother of God yet is ever more gloriously so as her Son is more gloriously the Redeemer of the World; nor has she ceased to be the chief participant in His Work of Redemption that continues through His Mystical Body, the Church, in the world, of which Mary is its highest and most honored member beneath its Head, our Lord Jesus Himself.

11

Mary and the Passion of Christ

THE "HOUR" WHICH JESUS told Mary had not yet come was, of course, His Passion, His supreme suffering as the Sacrifice for the sins of the world, the Holocaust of the New Testament, that would begin with His agony in the Garden of Gethsemane. As we have noted, it was Mary's choice, presented to her by her divine Son at Cana, to unite herself to Jesus in His Work, which He was about to begin with what would be His first public sign manifesting His divinity and culminate in His crucifixion at Golgotha. By agreeing, Mary unites herself to His suffering because she will suffer with Him—*and a sword will pierce your heart also*. What Jesus asked of her was not merely to accept what He was about to do, nor, still less, not to interfere; He asked her to unite her maternal heart to Him in a new way, to enter into His Sacrifice to His Eternal Father by willingly offering her Son and thus, through Him, herself for the world. He invites her to enter this way into His Passion, and thus, in a real sense, to share it, as only His mother can, who to Him is uniquely related naturally and spiritually. They will be separated until His Crucifixion when, although with Him, she will be unable to comfort Him as she once could. But in uniting herself to Him in this new way as a kind of co-redemptrix consonant with her role in the Incarnation as the New Eve, Mary will enter into the Mystery of Jesus' Passion, allowing her to share in it; it is the incomparable privilege He offers her and it is her greatest desire to please her Lord. In all this, Mary enters ever further into the divine Life of her Son.

Where was Mary when her Son was in His agony in the Garden and then arrested and brought to trial before the Sanhedrin? We only know that she was not with Him; for Scripture is silent about where Mary was or what she was doing during this final night. But we may be sure that, as she was at the Crucifixion, at the foot of His Cross, when nearly everyone else had forsaken Him, that on the eve of her Son's execution, Mary was not somewhere cowering in fear or indulging in the consolation of friends and family. Rather, she was, I believe, herself alone and in agony sharing in the mystery of her Lord's Passion as Jesus Himself had invited her. According to the visionary, Anne Catherine Emmerich (1774-1824), who experienced visions of Jesus' Passion, Mary stuck as close to Jesus as she possibly could; she followed Him to the place of His trial by the Sanhedrin, waiting outside for Him; she was present to see Him scourged, and followed Him in the crowd watching Him carry His cross to Golgotha. Catherine Emmerich's visions[1] were private and are not believed to be necessarily genuine revelations of what actually happened, but they ring true.

Mary alone can share Jesus' Passion, because she alone has been part of His Life from the beginning, and especially because she has been part of the mystery of her Son's presence in the world. Her agony is not something apart from Jesus' agony, as would be the merely personal agony of a grieving mother. It is rather a participation in Jesus' redemptive suffering, because she wills only what her Son wills just as He wills only what His Eternal Father wills. This is the essence of her participation. As Jesus struggled in the Garden to give Himself as the Sacrifice for sin, so we may confidently imagine Mary struggling in her grief and sense of personal loss to give her Son for the world willingly in faith without reserve or misgiving, with her whole heart united with His. One could

---

1. Emmerich's visions of Christ's Passion were written down and published as *The Dolorous Passion of Our Lord Jesus Christ*.

say she had no choice. And, of course, she didn't in so far as it is a question of altering events at this point. But she still had to choose it as an *act of faith*. As an act of faith. Mary could embrace Jesus' suffering and thus participate in it. Without faith and the love of God, she would certainly have rejected it in a profound resentment of such a violation of her personal contentment. Such is the choice of every Christian in the teeth of suffering.

As a matter of pure speculation, had Mary been with Jesus in the Garden, she may have been unable emotionally to be with Him at the Cross. The sheer physical and emotional experience of seeing Him in His agony sweating blood may, we may suppose from a strictly natural point of view, have rendered her emotionally helpless, overwhelming any deliberate act of faith that requires an emotionally calm recollection. As I have supposed, Mary, like Jesus, prayed alone that night, willingly sharing in the solitary inconsolableness of His agony. Mary's presence at the Cross was at once a profoundly spiritual experience and an emotional one. But it might have been debilitatingly emotional had she not, as Christ did in the Garden, prepared herself in prayer for the Cross.

Mary's suffering is necessarily vicarious. But while Mary is removed from the immediate experience of Jesus' suffering and depends on her faith in and love of her Son and Lord, her participation is nonetheless genuine and felt. Mary herself could not suffer directly in her physical nature what her Son was suffering directly in His genuine human nature, which would certainly have overwhelmed her. She can only share in it vicariously. But her participation is real and complete, encompassing her totally in mind and spirit. Although Mary hasn't the capacity to suffer to the same *degree* that Jesus suffers in His agony in the Garden, her suffering is of the same *kind*. With Him she feels the horror of His imminent death, the terribly violent character of which was as familiar to Mary as it was to anyone of her time living under Roman Law, for crucifixions were a *public* spectacle. She too will feel every assault to His honor and purity of nature, which she shares in her own sinlessness. She will suffer with Him His heartbreak when she learns of His betrayal and abandonment by His friends. And she alone with her immaculate heart can enter into His unique spiritual agony of bearing alone in the infinite purity of His Sacred Heart as the Son of God the unimaginably immense burden of the world's sins since its beginning. From her deep faith and love, these realizations of Jesus' Passion, we can believe, battered her heart before she ever beheld Him in His final agony on the Cross when her heart like His was pierced as Simeon had prophesied thirty years earlier. Mary had to accept the fate of her Son in so far as she could not have prevented it. But it was not merely as a *fact* that she accepted Jesus' suffering and death; she, who said at the beginning "Let it be done according to Thy will," *embraced* it in faith and hope as the will of God with the same love that He did, Who said in His agony, *Not my will but thine be done.*

We speak of Mary's faith and may ask what faith did she need having known so intimately the Son of God all of His earthly life and with no sin to obscure her understanding? But Mary is not divine; even Her divine Son in His human nature was not immediately cognizant of all things (cf. Mt. 24:36). She knows Jesus' mission and fate and their necessity for the salvation of the world, but she does not necessarily understand it. She could not know how the supreme agony, humiliation, and death of God's Son will accomplish the salvation of the world or even how it possibly could. She must have grasped, though obscurely, from the Prophets and Jesus' own explanations to her His presenting Himself to God as at once priest *and* sacrifice for the sins of the whole race; but It must all have seemed to her *rational* mind an infamous failure and defeat, a contradiction of all she believed, and an insupportable disappointment. As we need faith and hope in the teeth of our own sufferings and the immense miseries of so many in the world, which present to our weak human comprehension a contradiction of God's love, so did Mary when faced with events she did not comprehend and could not change. Mary too is enveloped by the darkness that envelops Jesus when she hears His cry from the Cross of those words from the 21st Psalm, "My God, My God, Why has Thou forsaken Me?!" But in the darkness of her Son's Passion, Mary does not doubt, because her pure heart is full of the light of faith in the mystery of God's power and purpose and in the hope of the resurrection. The apparent contradiction of reason and sense cannot defeat Mary's faith, which God gave her as He gives it to all of us, as a gift of the Holy Spirit.

Love demands everything of Mary and she holds nothing back but fully accepts the Father's will for her Son and for herself and gives her whole self to her divine Son and through him to all mankind. Throughout Jesus' Passion, Mary could not be near Him physically; but she had never ceased to be united to Him. In the mystery of love, she is fully attentive to His pain and sorrow. In a very real sense, Mary's agony is not her own. It is not the suffering she certainly underwent in her natural maternity as a mother who watches her son die and is thus no small part of her identification with Jesus' agony. It is rather in her mystical union with the Son of God Who is suffering for all men that she suffers most. How can something which, from the purely human point of view, seems so abstract and (rationally) incomprehensible overwhelm her natural emotions as a woman and mother? In her relationship with her divine Son, Mary has passed far beyond the merely natural sorrow of "*My* son is suffering; *I* have lost *my* beloved son" "Woe is *me*!", etc. There is now nothing that is exclusively her own pain. Her own sorrow is subsumed in the sorrow of her Son; by a profound co-inherence, it is His agony she experiences.[2] And this ability to participate subjectively in Jesus' suffering is her unique privilege as the Second Eve in this moment of the New Creation as her Son "makes all things new"; it is the privilege of the purity of her immaculate heart. No one else, then or now, could share that with Him in the profoundly unique way that she did. How Mary could do this is not something understood in the natural order of things. It is a mystery in the order of Grace, which I will consider in the next chapter.

---

2. Marie-Dominique Philippe, *Mystery of Mary*, 184.

12

Mary at the Cross

THE CROSS IS THE culminating moment of our Lord's Passion, when He becomes the perfect Sacrifice for sins, the Holocaust of love, the supreme Victim of God's all-consuming mercy and justice, and Mary's presence there is of the greatest significance for our appreciation of her. Traditional Catholic devotion, as I have already mentioned, has her following Jesus to Calvary, but the Scriptures mention her to have been present only at the Crucifixion. While it is beautifully fitting to imagine Mary with Jesus while He carries His Cross to Golgotha, it is enough that she is with Him at His Sacrifice on the Cross. It is only St. John who mentions her presence there, because he is the first to realize its significance beyond that of a grieving mother wanting to be with her dying son at the end; for John is the one to whom Jesus entrusted the care of His mother: *When Jesus saw His mother and the disciple whom He loved standing near, He said, "Woman, behold, your son!" And then He said to the disciple, "Behold, your mother!" And from that hour, the disciple took her into his home.* (Jn. 19:25-7).

Mary's presence is demonstrative of the mystical unity between her and Jesus. She is there not simply to be a grieving witness to, but to share in the suffering and Sacrifice of the Son of God, Whom she by the Love of God brought into the world. He came into the world through her, the perfect and willing instrument of God, His lowly handmaiden; so it is profoundly fitting and *important* that she would be there at His Death, still God's handmaiden, to participate in His Redemption of the world for which He came into world. She could not effect the Redemption nor offer herself as the Sacrifice for sins, but only to share and participate in it which was her supreme privilege and desire by a mystery of the Divine love that consumed her.

In his letter to the Colossians, St. Paul says, "Now I rejoice in my sufferings for your sake, and fill up on my part that which is lacking of the afflictions of Christ in my flesh for His body's sake, which is the Church" (1:24). And to the Romans he wrote, "Now if we are children, then we are heirs—heirs of God and co-heirs with Christ, if indeed we share in His sufferings in order that we may also share in His glory" (8:17). Now this in a uniquely profound way is precisely what Mary was doing with Jesus at Calvary. The experience was unique to Mary, but the *possibility* of it is not unique to her. Mary was there to bear Christ's sufferings, taking them into her heart and soul; so fully and powerfully did the love of God possess her; but she did what we do (according to St. Paul) in our own suffering when they are offered to the glory of God. By a mystery in the order of grace, Mary actually participated because of the sinless purity of her heart in the redemptive sufferings of Christ to a degree that even St. Paul could not. Thus, as the Holy Spirit through St. Paul revealed, Mary helped to complete what is "lacking" in them. But let's be very clear what we (and St. Paul) mean. Neither Mary, nor the Apostle Paul, nor any of us could complete Christ's Work of Redemption, because, first of all, Christ's Passion lacks nothing to accomplish the Redemption. It is a finished work, which Christ Himself accomplished, and which only he could. But *as a finished Work*, our Lord can and does ask us, as He asked Mary at Cana, to participate in it. In the natural order and in the order of reason, this makes little or no sense; but in the order of Grace, the order of love, it makes perfect sense. There is indeed nothing lacking in Christ's Passion except *our* share in it. It is a paradox that what is perfect in itself bids us to complete it by sharing it. The participation of each of us is the one thing it "lacks", because God will not compel any one of us when he or she *will* not. Mary was not asked to shed her blood with Jesus nor be tortured as He was, for it is not in physical suffering itself that we share in Christ's Passion but in the soul's *consent* to "add" our sufferings to His, outside of which they have no ultimate purpose or meaning. Mary of course consented and in the purity of her faith lived the mystery of her Son's Crucifixion and death. It was thus, as in everything else in the order of Christ's Redemption, that she was the first, leading the Way to Him Who is both the Way and the Destination, as St. Augustine famously put it.. So is Mary accorded the "highest honor of our race."[1] This was said of the great Old Testament heroine, Judith, who prefigures Mary as do a number of others in the Old Testament Scriptures (see Appendix B), for she is extolled as God's "handmaid" and "a God-fearing woman, serving the God of heaven night and day" (Judith 11:17), was blessed with words similar to the angel's salutation to Mary in Luke's Gospel: "Blessed are you, daughter, by the Most High God, above all the women on earth" (Judith 13:18), and praised as "the glory of Jerusalem, the surpassing joy of Israel" (Judith 15:9)[2].

When Mary hears her Son cry, "My God, My God Why has Thou forsaken me!." we can believe she is borne ineluctably into the heart of Jesus' Passion, her total abandonment to God of all hope and joy and even faith. For those words from the Son of God must have shattered any natural complacency however profound. Mary's faith and hope were in her Son as the hope of her people, Israel; He Who was to reign over the House of David forever had become accursed, publicly crucified as a criminal. She understood Him and His mission better than anyone else, but even so she could not without the profoundest suffering sustain the brute force of these facts. To remain true to the Father's will like her Son was a heroic act of faith. What Jesus' apparent utter defeat and dishonor required of her faith was beyond any formal understanding her religion could give her; only the life-long cultivation of her love of God in her divine Son by the Holy Spirit could sustain her in the teeth of such devastating experience. Mary's faith went far beyond

---

1. Judith 13:8
2. See also Judith 16:13-14.

the exterior circumstances which exceeded her mere understanding. So she went and stood beneath the cross of her Son to watch Him suffer and die, because against all her natural horror and anguish and doubt she believed that here and now He was making all things new, that He remained supremely Israel's and all mankind's Hope. Mary could have then in her sorrow and hope spoken the words of St. John, who was with her at the Crucifixion, written much later: *He came unto His own and His own received Him not; but as many as received Him to them gave he [the] right to be children of God, to those that believe on his name* (John 1: 11-13). It was the Father's will that it should be so, and Mary stood firm in His will, believing in His Love and His power. Thus could she accept the death of her Son, not merely the fact of it, but its full reality in the grace, power, and love of God. And thus did she cooperate and so participate in the redemption of man, becoming by her faith as the New Eve the mother of all who likewise believe in her Son, the eternal Son of the Father, Who first chose her to be the Mother of God and ours in the order of Salvation.

This is Mary's fruitfulness, her immense spiritual fecundity. We who love God, who are the children of God are her children in faith and this is why she has always been so highly honored. And thus did God reward her for her pure, uncompromising faith. But Mary's reward is not without precedent. God did the same for Abraham, whose faith prefigured Mary's, rewarding his faith demonstrated by his willingness to sacrifice his son Isaac simply by the Lord's command without understanding or asking why. Abraham's reward was to become the father of God's Chosen people, which included not just the Hebrew people but eventually, in Christ (prefigured in Isaac) the redeemed of the entire human race. Abraham's faith only prefigures Mary's because hers is the perfection of faith in God's Love and Mercy, hers was the culmination of the faith of Israel. For Mary not only cooperated with God to bring Him into the world, but too she cooperated in His Sacrifice for its salvation. Abraham was willing but did not have to lose his son; his was only a trial and but a figure of the Sacrifice of Christ. But Abraham's faith was fully realized in Mary who *with* her Son, Who offered Himself, offered Him to God for the world. It was the profound burden of Mary's faith and her participation in His Sacrifice to relinquish her Son at the Cross, which she faithfully did by her supreme but silent *fiat* or "Yes" to God, given most profoundly at the Annunciation and thence throughout her life. By her silent and sorrowful fiat at the cross, Mary accepted in her divine Son's crucifixion and death the contradiction of all that she best understood. Such faith is surely greater even than Abraham's. And to the extent that Mary's faith was greater so has been her reward, to be the Mother of all the redeemed in Christ, not merely in the natural order as Abraham was made father of a new race who would be God's People, but a new mankind[3] in the order of Grace to be raised to eternal beatitude in the very Life of God.

At the Cross, Mary's heart is possessed by the Love of God. And as the Cross reveals the heart of Divine Love, so Mary is at the heart of that Love. God in His infinite Love gave the world His Son through Mary and that could only mean that Mary, far from being (spiritually) a passive instrument, would be willingly consumed by His Love and thus herself an expression and gift of it to the world.

When Jesus saw his mother, and the disciple whom he loved standing near, he said to his mother, 'Woman, behold, your son!'. Then he said to the disciple, 'Behold, your mother!' (Jn 19:26-27). These words of our Lord from the Cross had the greatest significance for Mary as they did for John. To understand them we must see John as representative as a prototype. He is the only disciple to remain with Jesus to the last. Thus, John by his faithfulness represents for all time all who are faithful to Christ, who are the offspring of the New Adam Who redeems them by this His supreme act of obedience to God, the seed (His blood) by which He engendered the Church, all those who are thereby the adoptive sons of God. At this focal moment in the world's history, our Lord's gesture is not to be understood as merely personal. Jesus here is not acting only as a loving son who in his dying moment thinks of providing for his mother's welfare. No, Jesus is acting here in this eternal moment in the history of the world as the Son of God and for all time for the welfare of His Church. So, being entrusted with

---

3. See. Romans 6:6; Ephesians 2:15; 4:22-24; and Colossians 3:9-11.

Mary and taking her into his home, John is acting not in simple "charity", providing for a helpless widow, the mother of his Master and friend; rather, but is by the *caritas, the agape* of the Son of God receiving the Mother of God who is also Mother of the Church which her Son brought into existence as she did her Son.

Mary is considered to be Mother of the Church because Jesus has not only given her to John, but John to her—"Behold, your mother". By this eternal act, Jesus gives to the Church His mother, the New Eve and thus in a true sense co-redemptrix with Him as the New Adam in redeeming mankind and engendering the Church. He gives her to the Church, to all the faithful whom He has redeemed and He gives them to her. In this as in all her Son has asked of her Mary joyfully and painfully obeys. Joyfully, because it is her joy to please Him; painfully, because she is being asked once again, for the last time because His work is finished, to abdicate her maternal rights to her Son at the moment when she in her natural motherhood wants Him most as He was—so it seemed if not to faith, then to all natural feeling—to be about to leave her forever. Her maternal privilege is to have Him in His last moments all to herself; as His mother she is entitled to Him exclusively. But Jesus is giving her away. Mary is being raised, commissioned to, a degree of participation in God's work of salvation she hardly yet understands or is fully prepared for. But here too in the purity of her heart she consents, embraces the suffering it entails as her Son embraces His. And in "losing" Him she gains everything. In letting go of her Son, Mary becomes the Mother of all He redeems.

We see here yet another stage in Mary's cooperation and participation in the Redemption. From the Annunciation to the Crucifixion, she is being drawn with every act of obedience to God into an ever-deeper participation in His work of Salvation. Mary is being elevated, though it is still beyond her thought, into something far greater than her natural self, ascending into a new life that will culminate, as it will for all who love God faithfully, in the perfect union with and enjoyment of God.

13

Mary and the Resurrection

IT MIGHT BE SUPPOSED on the face of things that after the Crucifixion Mary's role was at an end, that there was nothing left her for to do. Her Son had left this world and left her behind. Mary has of course friends and family, but she has so closely identified herself with her Son, with His Person and mission, that without Him that it is likely she suffered a sense of being incomplete and without a purpose. Yet Mary knew of and believed Jesus' promise and prediction of His resurrection so that she suffered no loss of faith, only the challenge to it. What is more, Mary hasn't less to do with our Lord, but qualitatively (so to say) even *more* to do with Him. As Jesus has assumed His place at the right hand of the God the Father, so it follows Mary has too been raised to a new height in her relation to Him, which neither death nor any physical separation can sever.

As Mary's relation to the Son of God as the New Eve has flowered and flourished, she remains and is still more so the Serpent's, Satan's, fiercest enemy. This is so because she is no longer in a merely personal relation to Him (in one sense, she never was). To "crush the serpent's head", to free the children of Eve from the Enemy's tyrannical domination, as her "seed" (offspring) would do, required a greater role for her than simply that of bearing the

Son of God; and to enter ever more completely into that role, into an ever more perfect union with her divine Son, is Mary's whole future, culminating in her becoming, as St. John saw her in his vision, "A woman clothed with the sun, and the moon under her feet, and on her head a crown of twelve stars" (Rev. 12;1). But these reflections take us a little ahead of the immediate course of events after the Crucifixion.

Before Jesus' Resurrection, there is, of course, His burial or entombment. And this for Mary is the ultimate separation from her Son. In one way, it is even more painful to her maternal heart than the Crucifixion. At the Cross she could at least physically be near Him; and, after being taken down from the Cross, she could care for His disfigured corpse, prepare it for burial—the sad but real consolations of the bereaved. But once laid in the Tomb, He is inaccessible to her; she can see and touch Him no more. Now more than ever her sorrow must resort to her beleaguered (though not diminished) faith. While she still had His body to care for, He was yet physically "present" to her, but even this mere physical presence of His remains is denied her when His body is taken away to the Sepulcher. We must imagine Mary after the Crucifixion to be emotionally exhausted with grief and feeling very keenly the natural jealousy of a bereaved mother for the body of her beloved Son being taken from her, the body she miraculously bore and tenderly cared for. It is now being hurriedly prepared for burial—no lingering, no time for a luxurious grief—for the Sabbath is nearly upon them. But Mary doesn't refuse or complain; she accepts humbly the Law's demands upon the body of her Son as God's will in the same spirit she did when at the beginning of His life, not standing on any sense of superiority (however genuine) in her Son or herself, when she presented Him in the Temple. The days of separation in the Tomb are the last dregs—her final heartbreak—of the cup of sorrows which Mary has received willingly from her Son, a cup now drained. But Mary's sorrow will be turned to joy.[1] Her sorrow, born of her perfect faith, hope, and charity, will bring her into a deeper union with Her Son, Whose majesty as the eternal

---

1. See Jn. 16:16-22

Mary and the Resurrection

Son of the Father, will be fully borne in upon her at His glorious Resurrection and Ascension.

For Mary's heart this separation from Jesus was not a static moment, a "lifeless passivity" of *merely* enduring the heartbreak of it. She was also intensely waiting in unwavering hope of the promise of Jesus' Resurrection. And this waiting in the extreme poverty of her loss enriches and renews the intensity of her love of God in His Son. It is a silent blossoming of Mary's heart. For in her obscurity, which she had embraced throughout Jesus' adult life, quietly diminishing by all appearances in importance as her Son grew in His, Mary enters still more deeply into the mystery of her union with Her divine Son, to Whom she clings in faith, though His body is lifeless and buried, in the fixed hope of His triumph over death. Mary experiences in her loss precisely what the faithful Christian experiences: hope in the hidden Christ (He is also physically hidden from us), trust in His power as the Son of the Most High. We too as Mary did, though less perfectly than she, cooperate by grace in the mysteries of the Cross and the Resurrection.

Thus did Mary pass through the sorrowful mysteries of her relation to her divine Son, His Passion and Crucifixion, death, and burial, as she did through the joyful mysteries of His life with her. She is now prepared to enter into the deeper and higher relation of His new life in which she, but now no longer only she, will enjoy through the glorious mystery of His Resurrection. This deeper and higher relation Mary now enjoys with her Son is the fruition of that which began with and in her as the New Eve, as the mother of a new creation in Christ.

After the Resurrection and Ascension, Mary's own presence, almost despite her new role, has become still more obscure or hidden than before. For she is not mentioned again in Scripture until Pentecost in the Acts of the Apostles, when the Holy Spirit descends upon her and all the disciples, who are her children in the new creation, the brothers of her Son.

This silence about Mary is due to Mary's own silence. She has been retreating all along ever since the Wedding at Cana into the background of her Son's work. She is now wholly in the background. She is still the Lord's handmaiden, waiting upon His will alone; and so does not put herself forward, asserting her rights or her influence as the Mother of the Lord (think of what she might have said or done on her own account!). Certainly, Mary does not see herself in her role as the New Eve; she is not conscious of it at all. She is unaware of her own significance in her relationship to Christ; but her mind and heart are indeed wholly taken up with her Son and God's will for her in relation to Him. "Do whatever he tells you", she told the wine steward at the wedding feast at Cana, which expresses the sum of what was Mary's entire sense of her purpose and significance. She was and (whatever else she is by God's grace) is forever God's handmaid, pointing us to the same obedience to her Son.

Thus is Mary, though present throughout the events after the Resurrection, hidden in the obscurity of her own silence. Her silence is the silence of one patiently yet eagerly and thoughtfully waiting; she is waiting for the return of her Son, to be reunited with Him. And although now the conditions of their relations have changed (they have been changing all along), one thing has never changed: the perfect union of Mary's pure, immaculate heart with the sacred divine heart of her Son and Lord. Mary is living a wholly contemplative life, and thus a passive life of waiting for her Lord in prayer, thought, and recollection.

It may be helpful to understand Mary's attitude by comparing her to Mary Magdalene's at the Resurrection. The state of Mary Magdalene's heart is a confusion of sorrow, misgiving, and eagerness. She is the first to arrive (*before* dawn) at the Tomb when the Sabbath ended to anoint Jesus' corpse.[2] It is her eager wish to honor properly Christ's body with a complete anointing, because its initial preparation for burial had to be done so hastily due to the impending Sabbath. This eagerness to be doing something for Jesus is a beautiful and noble gesture of her love, but her love is all nerves, energy, and emotion with a mind yet wholly unrecollected. It is the same kind of busy, impulsive, passionate generosity Mary Magdalene shows when six days before the Passover at Bethany

---

2. See Jn. 20:1.

she extravagantly anointed Jesus' feet and then wiped them with her hair, for which Jesus praised her while gently chiding the energetic Martha for her different but less attentive kind of generosity.[3] While Mary Magdalene had chosen "the better way" than Martha, even her devotion is yet—inevitably—inferior to Mary's, whose intimate union with Jesus as His mother and through Him to the Father, and given the perfect purity of her soul, cannot have its equal. This is why it is easier to identify with Mary Magdalene (or with Martha), a great sinner and penitent who comes to Jesus from her need of mercy.

Now when Magdalene had rushed to the tomb (Jn. 20), she found two angels there, who were "dressed in white", but she was so distressed and distracted she didn't recognize them for what they were (she doubtless would have spoken to *angels* rather differently than she did) and we imagine she is rather put out with them for apparently being of no help to her but can only ask her why she's weeping, which must have seemed to her in her state of mind a rather stupid question. Nor did she recognize Jesus Himself when He appeared to her a moment later. It is obvious, I think, that she had not been thinking of the promise of His resurrection, but only of having lost Him and now of losing His body—"They have taken away my Lord and I don't know where they have laid Him" (v.13). It is true, Jesus appears to her as the gardener; but that is her mistake. Jesus isn't in disguise; she *supposes* Him to be the gardener (v.11). Magdalene was not looking for the living Christ, but the dead one. She undoubtedly loved Jesus, but she had as yet no understanding that He was more than a man, despite His God-given power and authority. Magdalene's love, though generous and devout, was still less directed by faith than emotion.

Mary, however, unlike Magdalene, remains in the background, hidden. She doesn't hurry to the empty tomb; she doesn't need the evidence of her senses to believe in her Son's resurrection. It came as no surprise to her as it did to the others. They never formally doubted His promise to rise from the dead, but neither were they *waiting* for Him as she was. Mary's love, though she feels

---

3. See Jn. 12: 7-8.

deeply all the normal emotions of grief and loss, is yet undistracted by them. Her love, by virtue of her sinlessness and her profound union with her divine Son developed over many years, penetrates far more deeply into the heart of Jesus' true identity and never loses its attentiveness to God's will either for her or Jesus, His Son. Magdalene's love for Jesus takes her only to the periphery of the mystery of Who Jesus is and what He has done. Mary's perfect love of God takes her into the very heart of that mystery and has drawn her further up and further in ever since the Holy Spirit first came upon her and she felt the first motion of the divine Life in her womb. And in her recollected silence, Mary has lived by this mystery, always so obscure to her mind, but to which her pure heart had by faith ever remained faithful. Mary doesn't seek Jesus in the Tomb either to honor His corpse, as Magdalene is intent on, or even to confirm His absence from it as the Apostles are in hurry to do.[4] Rather, Mary *waits* for Him.

Mary has lived in the mystery of His Birth, His life and mission, His Passion, and now in His Resurrection. She doesn't need signs of His resurrection to believe He has overcome death. It may be that Our Lord appeared to her and reassured her of His glorious new life or it was in some other way revealed to her. Or perhaps neither of these possibilities. Scripture is silent as is Mary herself. But I rather think she needed no special revelation to believe. Mary's wisdom and faith came from the contemplative depths of her union with Christ, not simply by virtue of being His biological mother, but in the Holy Spirit Who possessed her and from Whom she drew all her inspirations. And to put a still finer point on this distinction between Mary's and the Magdalene's love for Jesus: Mary no longer desired to be merely *with* Jesus, as was Magdalene's desire, but to be in some as yet indefinable spiritual way *united with* Him and *through* Him with God the Father. She reached that stage in the spiritual life, which Mary Magdalene was still far from reaching, in which she, at some level beyond the merely rational understood that Jesus was the Way to God, Whose

---

4. See Jn 20:3-10. This scene is depicted so well and famously by the Swiss artist, Eugène Burnand.

Son He was incomprehensibly, and that His work of redemption was to bring all men to Him and, further, into the mystery of their divine Life—*That they all may be one, as thou, Father, in me, and I in thee; that they also may be one in us; that the world may believe that thou hast sent me . . ."* (Jn. 17:21).

Wonderfully strange as it is to consider, when her Son at last rises from the dead, Mary is not there as she was at the Cross. To enter into the mystery of His Passion, she needed to be present at the Cross, to witness it; but entering into the mystery of His Resurrection was for her entirely a matter of a belief she already possessed. Not that Mary slept obliviously that night before the Resurrection; she no doubt kept vigil, waiting confidently for the power and glory of her Lord to be revealed.

Mary was waiting, but not just for the Resurrection as though it were an event unrelated to everything else she hoped for; she was waiting to be united still closer to her resurrected Lord, to share in His resurrection, to share fully His divine Life. Mary's pure heart was linked to Christ's in a way beyond any genetic or sentimental or even merely religious connection. Their hearts were bound by love, that is, the love of God, *caritas, agape*. Jesus, both as Man and, of course, in His divine nature as the Second Person of the Blessed Trinity, existed in the fullest beatitude of God's love; and Mary, through Jesus and thus by grace, was brought ever more fully into it. Mary's love of God grew through her knowledge of Him, which grew through her deepening knowledge of Jesus throughout her life. So now with her Lord having accomplished His great work of redemption, of which she knows herself to be a part, Mary waits to be, not *re*united with Him as Mother to son in the hereafter for that relationship has been transposed to a higher order where all things in the lower, natural order are to be renewed in Christ; she waits rather to be more deeply united to her Redeemer.

It is to be understood, what I have emphasized before, that Mary could not have expressed her expectation and desire in the way described here; for she lived this mystery of Her Son's Life and Death and Resurrection in her *heart* even while her *intellect*, with its inchoate knowledge of Christ (*theologically* speaking), could not participate. Mary *rationally* understood very little about the profound meaning of her Son's work and Person. It is always a mistake to suppose an abstract knowledge of God to be the same as that which comes by faith and the obedient love of God rather than by the abstractions of purely rational inquiry. We would be especially mistaken in Mary's case who had little abstract knowledge of any kind, having had no specifically theological education. But if simply educated, she was not simple-minded. Mary deeply understood her Son—far better than His closest disciples—yet not by a studied knowledge of the Torah (though Jesus must have answered a good many of her questions over the years as He had answered those of the temple scribes when a boy), but rather at a far deeper level at which their hearts were united: *Deep calls to deep at the sound of Your waterfalls; All Your breakers and Your waves have rolled over me.* (Ps. 42:7).

Mary's deep union with her divine Son was so intimate and so unutterably permeated by the love of God there was nor could have been any shadow of distrust or misgiving between them. In faith, hope, and charity, Mary was wholly oriented to God the Father through His now risen and glorified Son, absorbing her entire life. Therein was the source of her wisdom and her ability to enter into the mystery of Jesus' Resurrection.

14

Mary and the Mystery of the Ascension

ONE MIGHT BE INCLINED to think that when Jesus ascended into heaven forty days after His Resurrection, Mary once *again* had to be parted from her Son and that this was yet another painful moment in her life. And so it would seem from a purely human point of view. But Jesus' Ascension was a very different moment for Mary for at least two reasons. First, He had risen from the dead as He had promised He would and so was (very much) alive, to which Mary was no doubt a witness. Second, He was returning to the Father in triumph, having established His Kingdom, to begin a reign that will eventually encompass all of creation—*He that sat on the throne, said: Behold, I make all things new* (Rev. 21:5). Mary, we may be sure, understood what confused the disciples, that Jesus had not come to drive out the Romans and release the Jews from their political yoke to restore the Davidic kingdom. Mary had attended too closely to Jesus for too long to be under any such illusion. She knew that when Jesus returned to Heaven all would be different under a New Covenant in which all men could draw close to God. She was in no doubt that she would be again with her divine Son and that in some way she would share in the fullest possible way His new Life, which she better than anyone understood He was offering. She had His assurance of these things and their realization was her supreme hope.

Despite the absence in Scripture of Mary possessing this assurance, it is all but unthinkable that, during the thirty years of an increasingly profound intimacy between mother and Son, Jesus had not already directly offered her this hope. He had offered as much to His uncomprehending disciples. And if it is objected that this particular quality of Jesus and Mary's intimacy is itself without mention in the Scriptures, we might consider why any of the first three Evangelists would have been inclined to mention this intimacy any more than the many other intimacies of Jesus and Mary's life together which were, like this one, seemingly (to them) irrelevant to the instruction and life of the Church in their own time, which was their purpose in writing their Gospel accounts. This was not something they would have thought important. The Apostles' attention at this point, so soon after Jesus' Death and Resurrection, was properly taken up altogether with what He alone would tell them. The Church was yet to turn her attention to Mary's own significance and importance. John seems to be the sole exception. He alone seems to be keenly aware of this intimacy between Jesus and Mary. John is the only one of the four Evangelists who mentions the episode at Cana, into which he apparently had insights no one else had; and he alone mentions Mary's presence at the Cross. John's insights, especially as we have considered them, are very likely due to his own intimacy with Mary, with whom he lived for some years after Jesus' death. But, certainly, the other Evangelists had no such inclination as John to mention things into which they had no such insight.

Scripture is also silent about any contact between Jesus and Mary during the forty days before His Ascension. His appearance and interaction with certain of the Twelve and, as we've already considered, with Mary Magdalene, were recorded, but there is no record of any contact with His mother. This is at first puzzling even if we assume, as it is more than reasonable to do, that Jesus did visit His mother after the Resurrection. But, again, it is one of those intimacies that were not meant for the instruction or edification of the Church and so were left out of account. It is not difficult to understand why Jesus appeared to the Twelve, because there were yet things to teach them and prepare them for, namely their great apostolate as missionaries to the world and teachers of the Church. But neither was to be Mary's role in the Church. Unlike the Disciples and, as we saw, Mary Magdalene, Mary did not want to keep Jesus with her; rather, she wanted to be *with Him*: *And if I go and prepare a place for you, I will come again and will take you to myself, that where I am you may be also* (Jn. 14:3). Mary looked to the Ascension, the culmination of Jesus' Resurrection and thus of His entire work of Redemption. She was already in a *spiritual* relation to Jesus, a relation which had matured over the years but which the Disciples had hardly yet begun to enter into. It was a relation they hardly yet understood or anticipated, but of which the Holy Spirit would eventually enlighten them as He drew them ever deeper into that spiritual relation. Only one of them, John, known as the Beloved Disciple (i.e., he was especially close to Jesus), with whom Mary lived as Jesus requested at the Crucifixion,[1] had, no doubt, learned much from Mary and may account in part for the depth and simplicity of that Apostle's writings.

To be sure, the Ascension instilled hope in the ultimate triumph of Jesus' Kingdom and power over the world in everyone who believed in Him: *Men of Galilee, why do you stand looking into heaven? This Jesus, who was taken up from you into heaven, will come in the same way as you saw him go into heaven* (Acts 1:11). But Mary's hope was not primarily in Jesus' return in glory, but rather in *sharing* His glory, not as reward but as the culmination of a pure and perfect union with God in and through Jesus, His Son. She was not thinking, we may say, in terms of rewards or power or the Kingdom; the overriding object of her heart, of her faith, hope, and love, was Jesus Himself, the Eternal Son of God. Such was the purity and clarity of Mary's immaculate heart.

---

1. Catholic Tradition says that Mary lived in John's house at Ephesus for nine years.

The Apostles, I daresay, did not expect Jesus' sudden departure—*Men of Galilee, why do you stand here* [astonished] *looking into heaven?*. I should think they expected Him, now that He was clearly beyond the powers of the world, to stay and establish His Kingdom, His temporal and divine reign over his people and the world. It is, I think, equally likely that Mary was in no way surprised at the Ascension. She must have understood that Jesus' place was with the His Father—*Why were you looking for Me? Did you not know that I would be in My Father's house?* (Lk. 2:49)—as she herself longed to be with her Son and through Him united to God. She understood what the Apostles did not yet understand that Jesus' reign was infinitely more profound and encompassing than their conception of the messianic kingdom, that what God had accomplished in her heart, where He was enthroned and ruling all her desire, He would accomplish in the hearts of every one of His Children. And this He would do (could only do) at the Right hand of the Father where it is His purpose to bring us all into the same perfect unity, beginning with His mother who had already approached so near in her perfect faith and hope and love. Our Lord had made her the first, the glory and crown of His redeemed People.

15

Mary at Pentecost, the Descent of the Holy Spirit

ALL THESE WITH ONE accord were devoting themselves to prayer, together with the women and Mary the mother of Jesus, and his brothers. Here is the nascent, embryonic Church waiting for the Coming of the Holy Spirit Who would give her birth, by beginning in those assembled in the Cenacle (Upper Room), the divine life, communion with God in Jesus Christ at the deepest level of their being and giving them spiritual gifts that will sustain this Life in them and help them in turn communicate this New Life to rest of the world. And Mary is with them. She is with them because this is now her family in the New Order of Things that Her Son has brought about. But since God's first Advent into the world in her virgin womb, she has been living progressively this New Life through her intimate communion with Jesus Himself. So why, other than to be with her spiritual family at its incarnation, should she need to be there to receive the Holy Spirit with the others?

There are two apparent reasons. First, it is likely that the new spiritual community was gathered in the Cenacle *around Mary*, whom they doubtless revered and honored as the Mother of their Lord (who wouldn't have?) in much the same way that Elizabeth her cousin revered her when she acknowledged Mary as the "Mother of my Lord" at Mary's visit to her. They perhaps thought that to be near Mary, who had been so close to Jesus and was still close to Him, was to be in a way closer themselves to Jesus through her—yes, even the Apostles who had scarcely begun to live the inner life of communion with God. Far from presenting herself to them as such, they would have sought her out, no doubt and if for no other reason, on the strength of John's testimony of her wisdom and holiness. Mary's own example of prayer and hope in the divine promises must have been inspiring to them to wait patiently and pray fervently as we know they did. Mary, with her heart filled with the love of God, acted by virtue of her role as the Mother of God as, we might say, a 'midwife' to the Holy Spirit to bring about the visible birth of the Church.

Mary was already living the spiritual life and communion to which the Holy Spirit introduced the Apostles and the other disciples by coming upon them on that first Pentecost of the Church and thus knew better than they what the Holy Spirit could make possible for them and in them. In that knowledge she was, we may imagine, interceding for *them*, praying that by God's gift of the Holy Spirit they would perdure as one in Christ to the glory of God and the salvation of the world. Indeed, I imagine what Mary asked God for them in this vein was precisely what her Son had yet not, of course, in her own name but Christ's: *that they may all be one, just as you, Father, are in me, and I in you, that they also may be in us, so that the world may believe that you have sent me* (Jn.17:21). She wanted for them the same thing she had received from God, to be full with the fullness of His grace.

Yet Mary was prayerfully waiting in the Cenacle with the Apostles and the others for the same thing they were. The Holy Spirit came upon her too. This was Mary's final step that completed the divine work in her, total union with God. Although she had ever been under the *influence* of the Holy Spirit, she had not been till now *possessed* of Him. The Church (at least the western Church) has always understood and professed the Holy Spirit to proceed from the union of the Father and the Son in the Blessed

Trinity. And thus the Holy Spirit is, as one theologian expressed it, the "*nexus*, the 'tie' of the Father and the Son and [is] the One that [*sic*] unites us to the Father in the Son."[1] Although Mary received the Holy Spirit as did the Apostles, in her soul untainted by sin, her reception effected the same thing but to a unique degree. Mary's heart was already pure and had no need of the charismatic and spiritual gifts that would transform the Apostles and facilitate their mission in the world. She was already full of the love of God. She had at last reached the end of her pilgrimage toward perfect union with God. The Holy Spirit Himself was the ultimate gift of her spiritual life by which she would enter into that final mystery of God's life in her, the mystery of the Holy Spirit Who was Himself the Union of the love of the Father and the Son. Mary would live that mystery of Pentecost for as long as she remained in the world as she had lived all the other mysteries of grace to which God had been introducing her from the beginning. There is no explicit scriptural evidence of when Mary left this world, but it is likely that she did not remain long in the world after Pentecost, for after that there is no more mention of her in Scripture until she appears in St. John's vision in Revelation as the "woman clothed with the sun". But however long she remained, she lived in the silence of her humility and the all-consuming love of God that wholly enrapt her heart and mind. Protestants will find Mary's silence after Pentecost curious. After all, if anyone should have been exalted by the young Church as representative of God's grace it was Mary who bore the Savior. But her silence and humility, her hiddenness, is evidence of the spiritual poverty, which she chose and, I daresay, insisted upon for as long as she lived in the world. Mary's spiritual poverty was not the lack of communion with God but the willed abstention of anything that would distract her from it.

Mary needed no transformation, no charismatic gifts; she needed—desired beyond all things—only to be completely united to her Lord. And so what Mary receives from the Holy Spirit at Pentecost is a unique fullness of the divine life which the Holy Spirit had come to give and which the Apostles receive only in

---

1. Marie-Dominique Phillipe, O.P., *Mystery of Mary*.

its inception. At Pentecost, their intimacy with God only begins; Mary's reaches its full maturity. Mary's reception of the Holy Spirit is unique because she has a unique capacity with her immaculate soul to receive Him. To understand and fully appreciate Mary's reception of the Holy Spirit, we have to bear in mind that at Pentecost God did not bestow on the holy men and women in the Cenacle only a number of charismatic gifts, He was giving Himself to them to live *in* them, thus giving them a capacity to live the divine life in faith and hope and charity. In Mary this capacity already existed from her conception; at Pentecost it was *enlarged* to the fullest extent. She now could live in union with God, with the greatest possible (in this world) intimacy and intensity. In this way Mary's experience at Pentecost was unique. But this, I suspect, went unnoticed by the others.

Outwardly, Mary is one of the holy women praying in the Cenacle; inwardly, she is living a communion with the Savior the intimacy and intensity of which the others have yet scarcely conceived. In this way she is hidden even from them. Mary's inner life is wholly concealed, in part because it is still incommunicable, unutterable. And with the coming of the Holy Spirit it is even more so. Hence, Mary's silence and the silence about her in the Apostles' writings. Her poverty is in one sense a poverty of words and acts; her life has been becoming and is now wholly contemplative. And so Mary fades out of view and seemingly out of importance as the Apostles set about the tremendous business of building Christ's Church. But Mary's concealment is not a desertion; she is hidden *among* them, praying for the young Church and the world and thus sustaining them with a power few could guess—*the continual prayer of a just man avails much* (James 5:16). This she did in the same way as do now many men and women of contemplative religious orders (monks and nuns, so puzzling to Protestant Christians, hidden away as they are in remote monastic houses seemingly useless to anyone), who continually pray for the Church and the world and the enormity of the good they accomplish only God knows.

I want to digress here briefly to point out a fact about Mary that is often overlooked because it is so obviously true and because it has to do with her physical appearance, which is perhaps the least important thing about her, but in no way insignificant. The very obvious fact is that Mary *looked* so much like Jesus. The resemblance indeed must have been startling, given the fact that Jesus had no earthly father and so His genetic material came exclusively from Mary. He couldn't then have shared primarily any physical feature with anyone else. Of course, He may have, as occurs sometimes in children, taken after His maternal grandfather or grandmother rather than His mother. But I think that is unlikely. In any case, He doubtless resembled His mother more than any other child could. There is only one person, I think, Jesus could have looked like and in certain marked ways acted like: Mary. Seeing them side by side, No one could have failed to notice the uncanny similarities; the eye; the curl of the lips; the shape of the fingernails; something in the way each of them walked or held their heads in certain attitudes. Like identical twins, it is very probable that Mary and Jesus were (are) very strikingly similar in a hundred different ways. It may not be going too far to say that Jesus' human mind ran along the same tracks as Mary's; so that each often felt they knew what the other was thinking before anybody actually said anything as happens with some identical twins.[2] One striking inference from this fact is that the Apostles, who were so well acquainted with Jesus' ways and habits, must have been deeply impressed by this stark resemblance to Him in His mother. It is no wonder then that they revered her, seeing Him so clearly in her; nor that Mary never put herself forward, trading on, so to speak, so powerful an advantage.

Mary's continual prayer is for the Church, the members of which she loves with the love of God which she lives with a unique intensity and absorption. And because they are God's, she loves them as her own. She is uniquely aware that they were redeemed with the Blood of her Son. Her bond with her divine Son is a bond of love that encompasses the whole world but especially the *family*

2. I owe this very interesting observation to Father John Hunwicke.

of God who are united by the Holy Spirit in the Mystical Body of Christ. In this sense, Mary is not only the Mother of God but also ineluctably the Mother of the Church. Her intercession with its unique efficacy—before all others Christ listens to His Mother—upholds the Church, nurtures her. She is thus not a mere adjunct to God's love; she is the perfection of God's love enacted in the soul by the mystery of His grace in and for the Church through His Son. It is the same grace we all receive. So, Mary is not unique in this. Her uniqueness is in that she stands at the pinnacle in the order of grace and so is closest to God of all of His creatures; and in that propinquity is all her power and fruitfulness.

16

The Assumption and Coronation of Mary

THE ASSUMPTION OF MARY into Heaven is, like her Immaculate Conception, one of those Catholic Marian doctrines that are easily misunderstood. It is commonly supposed—and this by ill-formed Catholics as well as ill-informed Protestants—that Mary's Assumption is the same kind of event as Christ's Ascension. But there is a tremendous difference between the Assumption of Mary and the Ascension of Christ that reflects the essential difference (which should otherwise be obvious) between Jesus and His Blessed Mother: Mary *is taken* ("assumed") up into Heaven; Jesus goes there *under His own power*. Mary has no power of her own to perform such an act; it is by God's power and will that she is received body and soul in Heaven and that before the rest of us. As she had all along been advancing toward complete union with God, toward perfect beatitude, so far ahead of any other person in the Church, that the fact of her being raised body and soul into Heaven so soon before the rest of the redeemed, who will follow at the Resurrection of the Just, should not surprise and should present no serious difficulties. Protestant believers, who might otherwise allow for a certain reverence for Mary, find the very idea of her Assumption objectionable, because they labor under the false idea that the Church (even Heaven itself) is a kind of democratic or egalitarian society in which neither Mary nor anyone else enjoy any special distinction. But, were the Body of Christ egalitarian in this way, St. Paul's description of the Body of Christ in his first letter to the Corinthians would make little sense:

> For just as the body is one and has many members, and all the members of the body, though many, are one body, so it is with Christ . . . For the body does not consist of one member but of many. If the foot should say, "Because I am not a hand, I do not belong to the body," that would not make it any less a part of the body . . . But God has so composed the body, giving *the greater honor* to the inferior part, that there may be no discord in the body, but that the members may have the same care for one another. If one member suffers, all suffer together; if one member is honored, all rejoice together.[my emphasis] (12: 12—26)

Now, in the same passage Paul says that all parts of the Body of Christ are "indispensable" for each is a necessary part of the whole, possessing the same Spirit, Who makes us one in Christ. But he does not say the parts of Christ's Body are *indistinguishable* or undifferentiated. Each has its role according to his or her gifts. And in speaking of the spiritual gifts of the Church, St. Paul uses the unmistakable language of hierarchy:

> Now you are the body of Christ and individually members of it. And God has appointed in the church *first* apostles, *second* prophets, *third* teachers, *then* workers of miracles, then healers, helpers, administrators, speakers in various kinds of tongues. Are all apostles? Are all prophets? Are all teachers? Do all work miracles? Do all possess gifts of healing? Do all speak with tongues? Do all interpret? But earnestly desire the *higher* gifts. [my emphasis]

As there are different levels of the spiritual gifts to the Church and of their application in the external structure of the Church, that is, among her variously gifted members, it should not be difficult to believe that there are as well different levels of nearness to God of the *interior* life of her members. We all instinctively recognize this in someone who exemplifies to a very high degree the spirit of Christ. Mary's nearness to God has brought her to the very apex of spiritual ascent and nothing is more fitting that she be honored for it. When Mary Magdalene anointed Jesus' feet at Bethany, He insisted she be always and everywhere honored for her devotion: "in pouring this ointment on my body, she has done it to prepare me for burial. Truly, I say to you, wherever this gospel is proclaimed in the whole world, what she has done will also be told in memory of her."[1] It is easy to see the implication that if Mary Magdalene is to be honored for her act of devotion to our Lord, how much more should Mary, the Mother of God, be honored for her infinitely greater act.

It is also helps to consider that as God is supreme sovereign over all existence, He will do as He pleases with us, and justly: *I will have mercy on whom I have mercy, and I will have compassion on whom I have compassion.'* (Rom 9:15). It will be said that the honors paid to Mary are of human origin not divine. But it is universally agreed, and, after all that we have considered in these pages, obvious that Mary's participation in God's work of Redemption is unique; and if that be true, it is God's doing and He would not neglect to bestow on her proportionately unique honors. Yet what God did for Mary is precisely the *kind* of thing He will do for every one of His faithful; Mary is but the first in her preeminence as the Mother of God and all that that entails.

The question is often asked by Catholics as well as Protestant whether Mary died before she was assumed into Heaven. However interesting one may find the question, it is not important to the fact of her assumption. God took Mary body and soul into Heaven not so that she might escape death, but that she could intercede for the Church and the world.[2] Mary's intercession for us is to

---

1. Mt. 26:6-13

2. The idea of her Assumption being for the sake of her intercession for us is found in both the Eastern and Western traditions.

be understood in two operative senses: that she prays for us and that she *comes between* (in Latin, *cessit inter*) God and Man. She does this not, of course, *in place of* our Lord Jesus Christ, Who is in a very real sense her Savior too. She was so placed when by her *fiat* the divine Redeemer was conceived in her.[3] Once this simple and profound truth about Mary is recognized, there is little difficulty in further recognizing the collateral truth that her place between God and Man as the Mother of God is an *ontological* truth about her, that is, a truth about her very being, and that it is not a function *assigned* her by the Catholic Church. Mary was taken to Heaven to pray for us because it was to that end that the God gave her being; she was from eternity in the mind of God the *Theotokos* (Mother of God) and was thus realized by His creative utterance in the mystery of the Incarnation.[4] It should not surprise us that God should involve a mere human being in His eternal plan of redemption, not only because He took on His humanity within the womb and from the genetic material of the Blessed Virgin Mary, but also because He wills that all of His children of grace participate, to the degree He Himself makes it possible for any of us, in His work of redemption. By our own participation in His work of Redemption we are doing in our meager way what Mary did and still does by her powerful intercession, which is to bring His Son to the world and the world to His Son.

From her conception, Mary was prepared for her role, which she freely accepted, as the one to bring into the world God's grace through His Son. So, it is not so weirdly extravagant that she should be taken body and soul to Heaven to intercede for us. The standard objection to this belief is that Christ's intercession with the Father is infinitely sufficient. And of course it is. Mary's intercession is not necessary in the sense that God needs her. God *needs* nothing. He brought everything into existence *ex nihilo*, from nothing. No, God does not need Mary; He *chose* her; and, as a rational creature of free will, Mary chose *Him*. If Mary's Assumption and its purpose seem extreme, it is because it is the extremity of God's grace

---

3. See Fr. John Hunwicke's blog for August 16, 2016.
4. See Phillipe, *Mystery of Mary*.

and mercy to Man. By Mary's Assumption God demonstrates to the fullest extent what He intends with *our* cooperation to do for each of us at the Resurrection of the Just when He will give us back our bodies, *living* bodies, remade and incorruptible. And Mary by her loving intercession for us helps us toward this glorious end as we should be helping one another. Even in her glory in heaven, she remains the Handmaid of the Lord.

Mary thus is the first-fruits of the glorified Church. It is the same grace she received that she mediates to the rest of us still in this life, traveling along the same road to the same destination, who are still in our sins though free by grace from the guilt of Original Sin. But Mary's mediation is *in Christ*; and it is effective because it is by the power *of Christ*. As the New Eve, Mary is the first of the new creation in Christ. Thus, all the grace she obtains for us is in and through Christ. As with the creation, the Redemption is God's work; Mary only participates in it; and as the supreme participant, the Mother of divine Grace, she advances it, fosters it, nurtures it in all those who also love her Son. John Henry Newman, while still of the Church of England, wrote in his lapidary way of Mary:

> There was a wonder in heaven; a throne was seen, far above all created powers, mediatorial, intercessory; a title archetypical; a crown bright as the morning star; a glory issuing from the Eternal Throne; robes as pure as the heavens; and a sceptre over all . . .

The Coronation of Mary as "Queen of Heaven" in Catholic theology is for many believing Protestants perhaps more difficult than even Mary's title "Mother of God". But if we reflect for a moment, we may see that far from a sort of mystagogical idolatry as the Catholic Marian doctrine is usually accused of being by its critics, there is, as we have seen with her title "Mother of God", a certain inevitable and irresistible logic about it.

If we believe Mary to be the Blessed Virgin Mother of Jesus and Jesus to be the divine Son of God, the Second Person of the Blessed Trinity, and thus the divine eternal King, then is it not reasonable at least to suppose that Mary stands in relation to the Son in the divine order of grace as the Queen Mother as she would in any royal family in the natural order? It is thus a matter of historical fact that in the Davidic royal family of which Christ is the promised descendant,[5] Mary is the Queen Mother in the royal Davidic line.

But is it not carrying the point too far to call her Queen of Heaven? Let's first of all clear away some of the debris of long-held objections that still obstruct one's way to understanding this way of honoring Mary. There can be no question here of apotheosis, of *divinizing* Mary, of making her equal to her divine Son. It would be absurd to make her equal to Christ in being, since He is her creator. And if so, it is equally absurd to suppose Mary could be equal to her Son in *authority*.[6] If she is interceding for us in Heaven, she is not doing so by *imposing* her will on her Son. She *pleads* for us as an advocate and that only because she was *elevated* to that role by God in His infinite goodness for her sake *and for ours*.

It is because Christ as the Son of David rules an eternal, Heavenly Kingdom not a terrestrial one, that Mary His mother can preside as Queen of Heaven. The title is not therefore merely honorific. It bespeaks her real position in the order of grace. But she does not occupy that position by an ontological *necessity* in the same way that Christ does as King because He is the divine Son of God. Mary is a creature and an object of God's grace—*Hail, full of grace!* (LK. 1:28), which was made possible in the eternal order by the Sacrifice of her divine Son and made actual in time at her immaculate conception, by her having been conceived in the womb without original sin.

Although Mary as Queen of Heaven was declared a dogma of the Church as late as 1954 by Pius XII in his encyclical *Ad caeli reginam* ("To the Queen of Heaven"), this honor due her as the mother of our Lord was bestowed a early as the 4th Century by St.

---

5. He will be great and will be called Son of the Most High, and the Lord God will give him the throne of David his father, and he will rule over the house of Jacob forever, and of his kingdom there will be no end." (Luke 1:31-33)

6. Of course, the Protestant will regard this as absurd as will the Catholic, but it is as unreasonable as it is unfair to suppose as many Protestant Christians do that that is what the Church means by her veneration of Mary as Queen of Heaven.

Ephrem who called Mary "Lady" and "Queen", the title continued to be used by later Church fathers. Origen (died c. 254) calls her *domina* (Lady), the feminine of *dominus* (Lord). Mary is called the same by many other early writers, including St. Jerome, and St. Peter Chrysologus. And it was at the Council of Ephesus in 431, that Mary was declared dogmatically to be the Mother of God and thus the basis of her title "Queen of Heaven" was established. Mary's status was defined by the Council fathers in specific opposition to the opinion that Mary is "only" the mother of Jesus. Neither title may be supposed to have been a medieval invention, for they are titles almost as old as Christianity itself. "Queen of Heaven" is an honor due to Mary by right, but it is one that any Christian would wish to bestow upon her who considers Mary's certain and foundational role in God's Redemption of Man through our Lord Jesus Christ, and her perfect, loving obedience in serving Him to accomplish that redemption.

The Apostle Paul says of our Lord, "He became for us for us by God's power our wisdom and justice, and holiness and redemption" (I Corinthians 1:30). Mary then, *as* the mother of Christ, is the mother of our wisdom and justice, of our holiness and redemption, and as such is more our mother than our biological mothers; for she is our mother in a *higher order* of truth and of being. Our birth from her indirectly is our re-birth in Christ; from her womb is born He Who is our holiness, our wisdom, our justice, our sanctification, our redemption. Thus Mary's motherhood is not the mere occasion of an historical moment nor Mary herself a mere tool or a cog in a great machine or Process, but a servant of God, filled with His grace to participate in the great mysteries of His Incarnation and our redemption. And we who by the same grace also participate in those mysteries do so because she first did.

17

The Meaning of Mary's Virginity

MOST CHRISTIANS CAN READILY understand the importance, indeed the necessity, of Mary's virginity in conceiving the Son of God. But the Catholic Church has always insisted on her *perpetual* virginity. This is because the Church believes that Mary's virginity is an essential aspect of her sanctity. Even some Catholics will find this puzzling, for the Church also believes and upholds the sacramentality of marriage, which in Catholic theology means that marriage is not only a good in the natural order, but *as* a sacrament marriage is a means of *grace*. So, why does the Catholic Church believe that Mary's virginity was somehow special? Before answering the question of the meaning and importance of Mary's perpetual virginity, it will be necessary to answer some objections to the *fact* of her virginity beyond the conception and birth our Lord.

On the face of it, Scripture itself seems to deny Mary's perpetual virginity, but closer scrutiny tells otherwise. There are a number of passages in Matthew's and Mark's Gospels (Matt. 1: 24-25; 13: 55-56; Mk. 3:31; 6:3) that seem to evince unmistakably that Mary bore other children by Joseph. Many of these passages refer to the existence of Jesus' "brothers" and "sisters", although these English words are meant to do duty for the Greek word *adelphos* as found in the original Greek of the New Testament as well as the

Septuagint, the Greek translation of the Old Testament. *Adelphos* means "brother," but has a much broader semantic range than our English word.

Although in our English translations of these passages it may appear to be unmistakable that Jesus had natural siblings, before drawing any conclusions it has to be considered that neither Hebrew, Aramaic, or Greek, has a word to denote the relationship of cousin, and is therefore rendered "brother" in English or "adelphos" in Greek. But these words can mean a either a sibling *or* an extended relative. In the New American translation of the OT, for instance, the original is rendered "kinsman" or "relative." Even in modern English "brother" can be appropriately used to denote a non-biological relationship such as the members of a college fraternity or any other fraternal society. So, in the case of James, mentioned in Matthew 13:55 as one of the "brothers of the Lord", we know him to be a cousin or some distant relation. In Genesis 13:8 and 14:12, the word rendered "brother" denotes another case of an extended relationship, viz., Abraham and Lot, who are uncle and nephew, calling each other (as translated) "brother." The apostle James whom St. Paul refers to in Galatians 1:18-19 is the son of Zebedee not Joseph. There is some doubt that the James Paul refers to is a different James, who was only loosely speaking an "'apostle', and not the James who was one of the Twelve. In any case, it has always been widely accepted among biblical scholars that James as well as Joseph, also identified as a "brother of Jesus" along with Simon and Judas, were the sons of another Mary who, apparently like a number of Jesus' extended family, was a disciple of the Lord and whom Matthew calls the "other Mary," careful to distinguish her from the Mother of the Lord.[1] The Scriptures leave us no convincing evidence of Mary having borne any other children and the testimony of the ancient fathers of the Church uniformly confirms that Mary retained her virginity throughout her life.

Like every other attribution to Mary in Catholic Marian teaching, her perpetual virginity is not, as some think, an invention of the medieval Church. As early as the 4th century, there

---

1. See *Catechism of the Catholic Church*, 500.

is a good deal of testimony to an ambient belief in Mary's perpetual virginity. The Greek word, *aeiparthenos* ("ever-virgin"), had already been coined by the 4th century to express the belief. And as far back as the 6th century, Mary's perpetual virginity had been declared a teaching of the Universal Church at the Council of Constantinople II (553-554) which twice referred to Mary as "ever-virgin (*aeiparthenos*)."[2]

It may surprise many Protestant Christians that the great Protestant Reformers, Luther, Calvin, and Zwingli, all upheld the Catholic doctrine of Mary's perpetual virginity. Luther believed that Mary bore no other children nor had any marital relations with Joseph and averred that "it is an article of faith that Mary is Mother of the Lord and still a virgin . . . Christ, we believe, came forth from a womb left perfectly intact."[3] His 1537 Smalcald Articles refer to Mary in the terms of the Council of Constantinople, "Ever Virgin".[4] The perpetual virginity of Mary was Luther's *lifelong* belief; and even after he had rejected other Marian doctrines, he maintained Mary as the "Mother of God". Zwingli (1484-1531) and affirmed Mary's perpetual virginity: "I firmly believe that Mary, according to the words of the gospel as a pure Virgin brought forth for us the Son of God and in childbirth and after childbirth forever remained a pure, intact Virgin".[5] Calvin, though less straightforward in attesting Mary's perpetual virginity, was nevertheless "undoubtedly in favor of it":[6]

---

2. The Council only confirmed what was already believed throughout the Church. The early Christians had already coined the term *aeiparthenos,* "ever virgin", to express their conviction of faith, thus describing Mary's person in a unique and effective manner and denoting in a single word the Church's belief in her perpetual virginity. The word expression can also be found used in the second symbol of faith composed by St Epiphanius in the year 374, in relation to the Incarnation: the Son of God "was incarnate, that is, He was generated in a perfect way by Mary, the ever blessed virgin, through the Holy Spirit" (*Ancoratus*, 119, 5).

3. Luther, *The Works of Luther*, v.6, 319-320, 510.
4. See Campbell, *Christian Confessions: A Historical Introduction*, 150.
5. Zwingli, *Zwingli Opera, Corpus Reformatorum*, Berlin, v.1, 424.
6. *Encyclopedia of the Reformed Faith*, 237.

> It cannot be denied that God in choosing and destining Mary to be the Mother of his Son, granted her the highest honor ... Elizabeth called Mary Mother of the Lord, because the unity of the person in the two natures of Christ was such that she could have said that the mortal man engendered in the womb of Mary as at the same time the eternal God.[7]

Although Scripture does not explicitly teach Mary's perpetual virginity, the Latin, Greek, and Syriac Fathers had discerned its importance, for they repeatedly taught it. After all, St. Jerome in his treatise, *On the Perpetual Virginity of the Blessed Mary* (383), not only affirmed it, he defended it against those who in his own day objected to the doctrine. Many of those objections persist to the present day among those with misgivings.

Among these persistent objections are two that are outstanding. One is the reference to Christ as being Mary and Joseph's "firstborn" son. St. Jerome's plain and simple explanation of this apparent contradiction of the doctrine is that every only child is a firstborn child; and that it was Jewish practice at the time to offer sacrifice upon the birth of a "firstborn," without waiting for subsequent children to be born. The Greek word *prototokos* ("firstborn") is understood to denote a mere legal status and means only that there is no prior child and not that it is the first of a series (sometimes the equivalent ter *monogenes*, "only-born," is used). Also, under the Mosaic Law the term of "first-born" indicated the legal standing of the first male born without regard to any other children who may or may not have been born subsequently. So, there is no reason to suppose that Jesus being called in Scripture Mary's "first born" is meant to indicate the existence of other children born to her.

The other objection is inevitably raised as the reasonable inference to be drawn from Matthew 1:18 and 25, that Joseph and Mary had relations after the birth of Jesus. These passages refer to that period "before [Joseph and Mary] lived together" and to the fact of Joseph and Mary's having conjugal relations "until she bore

---

7. Calvin, *Calvini Opera, Corpus Reformatorum*, v. 45, 348.

a son." Although on the face of it is reasonable to suppose "until she bore a son" means that they had relations *after* she had Jesus, on closer inspection we see that Matthew here is merely noting that up to a certain point the marriage was not consummated. It is not meant to imply nor is there is any necessary implication that their marriage was sexually consummated later. St. Jerome cites in his treatise many scriptural passages to show that the phrase in question as used elsewhere in Scripture does not mean what it is often supposed to mean in the Matthew passage[8]. Let's consider just three of these passages St Jerome cites:

2 Samuel 6:23: *And Michal the daughter of Saul had no child to (until) the day of her death.* The obvious sense of this passage is that Michal was childless throughout her lifetime; any other possible meaning of "to the day of her death" would render the statement absurd.

1 Timothy 4:13: *Until I come, attend to the public reading of scripture, to preaching, to teaching.* Again, it can hardly be the case that St. Paul means for Timothy to attend to his apostolic responsibilities *only* until he (Paul) arrives and then stop.

1 Corinthians 15:25: For *he (Christ) must reign until he has put all his enemies under his feet.* To suppose St. Paul to mean what "until he has put . . ." normally indicates would be to make this proclamation not only heretical but nonsensical too. For Christ's reign is eternal and would be ridiculous if not wholly meaningless were it to end at the very moment He defeated all opposition to it.

It is natural to question whether Mary's perpetual virginity would make her marriage to Joseph unreal, even a kind of mockery of real marriage. Marriage entails the mutual right of husband and wife to the conjugal act of mutual self-donation. But a right may be possessed without being exercised. Mary and Joseph each had a right to the physical consummation of their union. But in so far as marriage is a union of *wills* to a common end of living a common life and raising a family (already provided for by God's

---

8. They include Isaiah 46:4; Matthew 28:20; 1 Corinthians 15:23-26; Psalms 122:2; Psalms 118:123; Genesis 35:4; Deuteronomy 34:5-6; Genesis 8:7; 2 Samuel 6:23.

miraculous intervention) to which Mary and Joseph each fully consented, their marriage was genuine without a sexual union. No one would say theirs was a normal or *usual* marriage, involving as it did the direct action of God, but neither can it be said to be a false one. One can imagine a man and woman choosing to marry despite an inability to consummate their marriage, because they desire a common life and hope for an adoptive family. Consent, not consummation, is "the indispensable element that 'makes the marriage.'"[9] Consummation is the *natural* outcome of mutual consent but allowing for unusual circumstances, as in the case of Joseph and Mary, it is neither necessary or inevitable.

Considering Mary's marriage to Joseph, it is necessary to understand the unitive nature of the conjugal act because it is the nature of the act that explains why Mary remained a virgin. Despite its common abuse as a casual and fruitless liaison for pleasure, the act of sexual union is the most intimate physical act of union between a man and a woman; as such it is a unitive act as well as a procreative one—*And the two shall become one flesh*. If marriage fundamentally requires the mutual self-donation of each person, their sexual union is the physical expression (not the only kind) of their mutual self-giving and children its natural result. Mary could not give herself to Joseph sexually, because she had already given herself, physically as well as spiritually, to God. But it is certain she gave herself to him in all other respects short of her devotion she owed to God.

---

9. *The Catechism of the Catholic Church*, no. 1626.

18

Mary's Past

ONE LAST THING ABOUT Mary to which I would like to introduce my Protestant reader is something that Catholic tradition tells us about her that is perhaps little known among Protestant Christians (and many Catholics) and which perhaps can enhance our understanding and appreciation of her. This is that Mary had been consecrated to God since she was a very little girl. We learn from ancient tradition as related in early Christian literature[1] that from the age of three Mary was consecrated to God; that her parents, Joachim and Ann, had dedicated her to the Temple to be reared and educated. Mary belonged to what biblical historians suppose to have been a school of virgins in the Temple of Jerusalem that formed a sort of altar guild which performed all the tasks of maintenance for the Temple rites. These would have included such things as sewing and creating vestments, washing the vestments of the priests, preparing liturgical linen, weaving the veil of the Temple, and, most importantly, liturgical prayer. Both the Jewish and Catholic traditions hold that the Israelite virgins of the

---

1. It is recorded for instance in the *Protevanglium* of James, an apocryphal book of the 2nd century. Although not canonical, the book bears witness to the ancient traditions of the Christian faithful regarding the Blessed Virgin Mary, as well as other beliefs common among the first Christians. Cf. http://taylormarshall.com/2011/12/did-jewish-temple-virgins-exist-and-was.html.

Temple school completed their service and training by marrying age (about 14) and that they were dismissed at this time to (presumably) enter into a normal social life, namely marriage. Older women may have been a part of the school as well, widows like the prophetess Anna, serving as teachers and governesses for the girls under their care.[2] Again, according to ancient tradition and the unanimous conviction of the Fathers of the Church, it was during the time of Mary's service in the Temple that she took a vow of virginity. Thus, it is believed that when Mary became betrothed to Joseph, she had been a Temple virgin for most of her life and had vowed to remain a virgin. St Augustine believed Mary's vow was evident from her being "troubled" at the Annunciation; for had she intended to be an ordinary wife and bear Joseph children, she would not have been so amazed at Gabriel's announcement; she found it difficult at first to understand that as she had taken such a vow in dedicating herself as a virgin to God,[3] And now God was asking her to bear a child. Certainly, Mary was *at least* as surprised by what God wanted of her in view of her avowed virginity as by the miraculous means by which He would fulfill it. But why, we must ask, if Mary had taken such a vow, did she become betrothed to Joseph in the first place?

First, there was nothing in Jewish law to forbid her marrying and that a celibate marriage was not incompatible with her dedication to God if her husband agreed to it. We must assume that Mary would have told Joseph before their betrothal that she intended to remain a virgin; no virtuous woman, let alone the Mother of God, would have so deceived her husband. Now if Joseph knew her intention and still intended to marry her, we may suppose that he agreed to a childless marriage. It almost goes without saying, but unless we suppose Joseph to have been unfaithful to Mary and

2. The Jewish historian Josephus mentions in Book 5 of the *Jewish Wars* that there were 'cloisters' in the Temple for (presumably) consecrated women to live there as servants of the Temple. There are also several biblical OT texts (in the Catholic canon) which together strongly suggest the existence of consecrated virgins in service at the Temple, viz., Ex. 38:8; I Sam. 2:22; 2 Macc 3:19-20.

3. See Augustine, *Works*, Sermon 225, 2

there is no reason to suppose such a thing, Joseph too, at least by virtue of marrying an avowed virgin, had himself to have vowed chastity for the rest of his life.

But why then did Joseph marry a woman whom he knew would remain childless and with whom he could not even enjoy the normal conjugal right of sexual relations? The only answer to that question is of course that he *loved* her and that Jewish law (or any other law) did not prohibit such a marriage unusual as it was. His love for Mary indeed transcended the mere rights of a husband to beget children and over his wife's body in sexual intimacy. Joseph then lived with Mary in a relationship that was not sexual but which was nevertheless intimate and loving—a true marriage, performing all the duties of a husband. It may be difficult to understand this of a man, but Joseph could not have been any ordinary man. Little is known about Joseph, apart from the apocryphal literature; for he has small mention in Scripture. Yet from the little Scripture does say of St. Joseph, we know that, besides being a carpenter, he was a simple (in the best sense) man of great humility and faith who loved God and was faithful to his religion, piously observing all that was commanded by the Law and more as God required it of him.

The marriage of Mary to Joseph was, therefore, not in the usual way normal; that is, it was not for the purpose of creating and raising a family. But when Mary bore the Christ Child, their marriage became "normal" with the object now of raising a child, but a Child Who, they understood was not "normal". Their marriage was certainly provident in God's eternal plan of Salvation to raise Jesus, Who was to be born into the world an infant and thus into a human family that like all families would provide all that He would need for His human development. That Jesus was not conceived naturally by the conjugal union of Mary and Joseph but by a supernatural union of Mary and the Holy Spirit, and was in His divine nature the Second Person of the Blessed Trinity, determined the uniqueness of the Holy Family and the blessedness of the relationship of both Mary and Joseph to God.

Mary's girlhood spent in devotion in the Temple was, we can see, consonant with her entire life. From her early avowed virginity as an expression of devotion to God and her service in the Temple came her willingness to do His will in *any* event, from His miraculous conception in her womb to the poverty and silence of the rest of her life.

Epilogue
So, What's the Point?

PERHAPS THE TWO MOST important things for anyone reading this book, but especially for the Protestant reader, to take away from these reflections on the Blessed Virgin Mary is that she is *one of us*, redeemed by God's infinite love and grace; and that Mary can only be understood and appreciated, her entire meaning and significance is, only in her relation to the Person and redemptive power of Jesus Christ. She is not a different kind of being—still less a kind of deity for, like us, she is nothing *in herself*—nor does the Catholic doctrine of Mary purport her to be. We are all born from Adam, so that Mary is our sister in the natural order. She is also our mother in the supernatural order of grace. She is our mother because, untainted by original sin by God's good grace, she bore Christ the Incarnate Son of God, Who, in His full and true humanity, is our brother. Thus, Mary bears to us a profound familial relation as does Christ Himself by His Incarnation. Christ as the New Adam makes all things new—*And He who sits on the throne said, 'Behold, I am making all things new'* (Rev. 21:5)—a new creation in which it becomes possible for all men, including Mary, to enter into communion with God by a new intimacy accomplished by Christ's Sacrificial Death, Resurrection, Ascension, and by the Gift of the Holy Spirit, an intimacy unknown even to our unfallen First Parents—"O happy fault!".[1] We now with Mary are *in Christ* and

---

1. This expression appears in the *Exsultet* of the Catholic Paschal Vigil Mass. The whole line reads, *O felix culpa quae talem et tantum meruit habere*

enjoy (although now only very imperfectly in our sinfulness) a familial relation to God, participating in the very Life of the Blessed Trinity in and through Jesus Christ. Mary was simply the first (and by no means the last) to enter fully into that perfect communion with God in Christ as we have in these reflections noted her to have done. If Mary stands in Catholic teaching at the pinnacle in the order of grace, it is not because she climbed to that summit, but because God placed her there by His grace to be a *means* of grace for those of us who would follow the same Way to God that she followed, i.e., through her love for Jesus Christ. Note well that Mary is a means of grace not a *source*. Grace does not originate from her but comes to us through her as our supreme intercessor among many intercessors in Heaven who would see us arrive at the same end that they are now enjoying. Mary is supreme because God has so honored her. Her glory is not her own, as something earned; she is clothed with the glory of God, "as a woman clothed with the sun".

From her conception, all that she has become has been given her in the order of grace, in the divine order of things, and all for the redemption of Man. Her very freedom from original sin was so that she could freely cooperate with God and, in so doing, freely participate in His divine Life into eternity. And her free cooperation was essential to her becoming the Mother of God. Mary was not compelled to become this exalted creature; she freely *chose it* by her saying "Yes" to God throughout her life, as much as God has chosen it *for her*. This is why, when Jesus wished to impress upon those of His natural family who would have His exclusive attention, that to be related to Him was now essentially not a matter of blood or biology but love and obedience, He said pointing to His disciples: *Here are my mother and my brothers, anyone who does the will of my Father who sent me is my brother and my sister and my mother* (See Matt. 12:46-9). God exalted Mary because she

---

redemptorem, "O happy fault that earned for us so great, so glorious a Redeemer."] Saint Ambrose (340—397) also speaks of the fortunate ruin of Adam in the Garden of Eden in that his sin brought more good to humanity than if he had stayed perfectly innocent.

did His will and prepared her to do so in her special role from her conception; she was at once the first of the new creation in Christ and was the primary instrument—the handmaid of the Lord—by which He made it possible. Thus in her *Magnificat,* Mary's hymn of gratitude, she says, *My soul proclaims he greatness of the Lord, my spirit rejoices in God my Savior . . . the Almighty has done great things for me . . . He remembered His promise of mercy He made to . . . Abraham and his children forever.* And we with her are the children of Abraham whom Christ has redeemed.

Mary is indeed one of us, but we are not her equal. When we think of Heaven or for that matter Christ's Church, we must free our minds of all our egalitarian ideas learned from our centuries-long in-bred democratic experience. We do well to remember that Christ is *King.* And it follows then that Mary is the Queen of Heaven. Thus has God exalted her. That He has done this is a glorious fact the Church joyfully acknowledges but did not invent. If to exalt a mere human being so gloriously is audacious, it is God's audacity not ours. No one would have dared to hope or even imagine for any merely human being what God has promised to us—what He has already done for Mary: . . . *eye has not seen, nor ear heard, neither has it entered into the heart of man, what things God has prepared for those who love him* (I Corinthians. 2:9). Certainly, all our notions and expectations of democratic equality and fairness are irrelevant in the order of grace. None of us are equal in relation to God, because we are not all equally near Him as we do not all equally love Him. We are all sinners of course; and we are all in need of His grace and mercy, which He does not refuse to any who asks for them. But as we receive them only to the degree that we seek them, we do not possess them equally. God invites us all to partake of the divine nature, to participate in the life of the Godhead in and through Jesus Christ (2 Peter 1:4), but by our own choice and acts we do not participate equally. Sanctification is necessarily a cooperation with God's grace; it is chosen and strived for not imposed. The work of grace when perfected will produce, as C. S. Lewis once expressed it, "a creature which, if you saw it now, you would be strongly tempted to worship."[2] Such is the glorious perfection of grace in the human person. To honor Mary as Queen of Heaven, then, is hardly strange or incongruous when one considers what God's grace will accomplish in any of us who fully participates in His divine life. By the Incarnation, the Eternal Word was eternally united with the nature of man and thus in Him is *all* mankind in a real sense deified, made to share in the life of the Blessed Trinity: "He was made man", says St. Athanasius (c.298—373), "that we might be made gods."[3] Mary, as I have said repeatedly, is the first fruits of the New Creation, the New Eve, not of our fall but of our redemption, and thus the first to enter into the Kingdom of God. And what is more fitting then that she be preeminent[4] who is at once by the mystery of God's grace the eldest daughter of the Kingdom and Mother of the King. Mary doesn't unite us to God; only Christ can do that; but she can aid and abet that union by her intercession on our behalf.

We must ever bear in mind about Mary that she always and ever specially belonged to God, selected by Him from her conception to be the Mother of His Son. Throughout her life, she was ever His devoted servant, His handmaiden, throughout her upbringing, marriage, and her entire adult life. She lived with Jesus in the intimacy of a mother and her son, then followed Him throughout His ministry, though in obscurity never insinuating herself, yet always nearby even at His arrest and crucifixion. And she is present still serving Him in His Church, ever a witness to His love and the power of His grace.

Mary is the first to enter fully into the life of God by grace and so she is the Mother of Grace to all those who seek likewise the grace of God. in Christ, we follow her in succession, sharing His Resurrection, toward full union with God, the Beatific Vision, the culmination of God's work of grace, which Mary already enjoys.

2. Lewis, *The Weight of Glory*.
3. Athanasius, *De Incarnation Verbi*, 54.
4. See Ps. 45:13-14.

Epilogue

She is the first on that Way which is Christ, Who honors her as Queen of Heaven not merely because she bore Him but because in faith she *obeyed* Him, making her Mother of all who are faithful to Him.

Because Mary was given the grace of an immaculate soul untouched by Original Sin, does not mean that her faithfulness to God was automatic, as though she were a kind of robotic servant with no will of her own. Being free of Original Sin is not to be without a free will. Mary's willingness to obey God and bear His Son as the New Eve was as free and voluntary as was the 'old' Eve's disobedience. If this were not so; if God had *made* Mary agree to bear His Son, as opposed to *making it possible* for her to do so, God's principal act of Redemption, the Incarnation, would have been an act of compulsion and as such would have rendered the essential character of our salvation likewise an act of compulsion. For in that case man could have had no real part in undoing the Fall as he unmistakably did in causing it. The Incarnation could still have happened, but it could not have had the same meaning. The Athanasian Creed expresses the meaning of the Incarnation in this way, "For the Son of God became man so that we might become God."[5]. God became Man that we could participate in His Godhead, in His essential life. But our participation would be meaningless if it were an *un*willing act. Christ's own obedience to God, as the New Adam, would be all but meaningless and inconsequential in so far as we could never, as St. Paul enjoined us, *imitate* Him (Ephesians 5:1). We must, as Mary did, *participate* in our salvation.

But if Mary can mean anything to us; if she is to be honored as the Church since antiquity has honored her, as Queen of Heaven, Mother of Mercy and Mediatrix of the Graces of God, the New Eve, etc., it is only because she is first our sister, like us born of Adam, a daughter of Eve. Mary is what we, as Christians will

---

5. Athanasius, *De Incarnation Verbi*, 54, 3. St. Irenaeus (d. 202 A.D.) taught the same: 'For this is why the Word became man, and the Son of God became the Son of man: so that man, by entering into communion with the Word and thus receiving divine sonship, might become a son of God.' (Adv. haeres. 3, 19.). See also 2 Pet 1:4.

become by God's ineffable grace, if we, like her, love God with our whole being, kings and queens in the Kingdom of Heaven (Rev. 5:10). But she will forever have the primacy and the greatest honor among us in Christ, for He, as He remains eternally Man in His Resurrection, He remains eternally her Son and she His Mother and our Mother in Him Who gave her to us.

One last word about Mary's role as intercessor in heaven. I have emphasized that Mary is one of us, that she is no less the "product" of divine grace and shares necessarily in Christ's salvation. But what she has become in the order of salvation, the order of grace, is immensely more than just a woman, as all the faithful in Christ will become incalculably more than "saved souls"— again, to quote St. Paul: "as it is written, 'no eye has seen, nor ear heard, nor the heart of man imagined, what God has prepared for those who love him'" (I Cor. 2:9). If Mary is Queen of Heaven and, as such, is helping us gain the same blessedness she enjoys, it is because has God so honored her; and we should do likewise. To advance His purpose in the world, God uses those, who are willing (and sometimes the unwilling who are mere tools rather than servants) to be used by Him. When one prays for the good of another, as we are commanded to do, one is interceding to God for that other person. Mary's intercession does essentially nothing more or less, although hers is incalculably more effective because she is incalculably nearer to Him. Even so, many good Protestants may object that Mary's intercession for our salvation is wholly unnecessary and superfluous to Christ's own intercession for us; and that it is heretical to suppose the intercession of anyone else however holy could substitute for it or equal it. With this Catholic doctrine wholly agrees. The truth is, Mary *is* unnecessary; for no one is necessary to our salvation but God Himself and our freely choosing Him. But then, the Church has never taught that Mary's intercession should be considered adequate without Christ's. In Catholic theology such an idea is an absurdity. After all, He is *her* Savior too. No, Mary's intercession, as powerful as it is claimed to be, could never supersede Christ's; it can only share in it even if to a superlative degree. Mary has no voice or authority of her own—nothing she wields independent of God. As the very idea of Mary's intercession would be absurd without Christ, so then would every act of charity; for what could "charity" possibly mean if it does not participate in the divine Love. *Do whatever He tells you*, she told the stewards at the Wedding at Cana and *us*; for those are her last words recorded in Scripture and they express the whole purpose of her life and ours in Christ.

I conclude this book with a prayer for every Christian who with Mary loves Christ:

Eternal Father, Source of light in every age, Thou gave us the Blessed Virgin Mary, who by Thy infinite Love and Mercy conceived and bore Thy Son. May she help us by her intercession and her example of faith and love of Thee to love Thy Son as she loves Him and thus draw down on Thy faithful people all of Thy graces through all ages. Grant this, we earnestly ask Thee, merciful God, through Christ our Lord. Amen

Appendix A

WITH THESE CITATIONS ARE John Henry Newman's commentary.

1. St. Justin:

    "We know that He, before all creatures, proceeded from the Father by His power and will,...and by means of the Virgin became man, that by that way the disobedience arising from the serpent had its beginning, by that way also it might have an undoing. For Eve, being a virgin and undefiled, conceiving the word that was from the serpent, brought forth disobedience and death; but the Virgin Mary, taking faith and joy, when the Angel told her the good tidings, that the Spirit of the Lord should come upon her and the power of the Highest overshadow her, and therefore the Holy One that was born of her was Son of God, answered, 'Be it to me according to Thy word.'"

    -Tryph. 100.

2. Tertullian:

    "God recovered His image and likeness, which the devil had seized, by a rival operation. For into Eve, as yet a virgin, had crept the word which was the framer of death. Equally into a virgin was to be introduced the Word of God which was the builder-up of life; that, what by that sex had gone into perdition, by the same sex might be brought back to salvation. Eve had believed the serpent; Mary believed Gabriel;

Appendix A

the fault which the one committed by believing, the other by believing has blotted out."

-De Carn. Christ. 17.

3. St. Irenaeus:

"With a fitness, Mary the Virgin is found obedient, saying, 'Behold Thy handmaid, O Lord; be it to me according to Thy word.' But Eve was disobedient; for she obeyed not, while she was yet a virgin. As she, having indeed Adam for a husband, but as yet being a virgin . . . becoming disobedient, became the cause of death both to herself and to the whole human race, so also Mary, having the predestined man, and being yet a Virgin, being obedient, became both to herself and to the whole human race the cause of salvation.

. . . And on account of this the Lord said, that the first should be last and the last first. And the Prophet signifies the same, saying, 'Instead of fathers you have children.' For, whereas the Lord, when born, was the first-begotten of the dead, and received into His bosom the primitive fathers, He regenerated them into the life of God, He Himself becoming the beginning of the living, since Adam became the beginning of the dying. Therefore also Luke, commencing the line of generations from the Lord, referred it back to Adam, signifying that He regenerated the old fathers, not they Him, into the Gospel of life. And so the knot of Eve's disobedience received its unloosing through the obedience of Mary; for what Eve, a virgin, bound by incredulity, that Mary, a virgin, unloosed by faith."

-Adv. Haer. iii. 22.34.

And again:

"As Eve by the speech of an Angel was seduced, so as to flee God, transgressing His word, so also Mary received the good tidings by means of the Angel's speech, so as to bear God within her, being obedient to His word. And, though

Appendix A

the one had disobeyed God, yet the other was drawn to obey God; that of the virgin Eve the Virgin Mary might become the advocate. And, as by a virgin the human race had been bound to death, by a virgin it is saved, the balance being preserved, a virgin's disobedience by a virgin's obedience."

-Ibid. v.19.

Now what is especially noticeable in these three writers, is, that they do not speak of the Blessed Virgin merely as the physical instrument of our Lord's taking flesh, but as an intelligent, responsible cause of it; her faith and obedience being accessories to the Incarnation, and gaining it as her reward. As Eve failed in these virtues, and brought on the fall of the race in Adam, so Mary by means of them had a part in its restoration not to go beyond the doctrine of the Three Fathers, they unanimously declare that she was not a mere instrument in the Incarnation, such as David, or Judah, may be considered; they declare she co-operated in our salvation not merely by the descent of the Holy Ghost upon her body, but by specific holy acts, the effect of the Holy Ghost within her soul; that, as Eve forfeited privileges by sin, so Mary earned privileges by the fruits of grace; that, as Eve was disobedient and unbelieving, so Mary was obedient and believing; that, as Eve was a cause of ruin to all, Mary was a cause of salvation to all; that as Eve made room for Adam's fall, so Mary made room for our Lord's reparation of it; and thus, whereas the free gift was not as the offence, but much greater, it follows that, as Eve co-operated in effecting a great evil, Mary co-operated in effecting a much greater good.

And, besides the run of the argument, which reminds the reader of St. Paul's antithetical sentences in tracing the analogy between Adam's work and our Lord's work, it is well to observe the particular words under which the Blessed Virgin's office is described. Tertullian says that Mary

APPENDIX A

"blotted out" Eve's fault, and "brought back the female sex", or "the human race, to salvation"; and St. Irenaeus says that "by obedience she was the cause or occasion" (whatever was the original Greek word) "of salvation to herself and the whole human race"; that by her the human race is saved; that by her Eve's complication is disentangled; and that she is Eve's Advocate, or friend in need. It is supposed by critics, Protestant as well as Catholic, that the Greek word for Advocate in the original was Paraclete; it should be borne in mind, then, when we are accused of giving Our Lady the titles and offices of her Son, that St. Irenaeus bestows on her the special Name and Office proper to the Holy Ghost.

So much as to the nature of this triple testimony; now as to the worth of it. For a moment put aside St. Irenaeus, and put together St. Justin in the East with Tertullian in the West. I think I may assume that the doctrine of these two Fathers about the Blessed Virgin, was the received doctrine of their own respective times and places; for writers after all are but witnesses of facts and beliefs, and as such they are treated by all parties in controversial discussion. Moreover, the coincidence of doctrine which they exhibit, and again, the antithetical completeness of it, show that they themselves did not originate it. The next question is, Who did? for from one definite organ or source, place or person, it must have come. Then we must inquire, what length of time would it take for such a doctrine to have extended, and to be received, in the second century over so wide an area; that is, to be received before the year 200 in Palestine, Africa, and Rome. Can we refer the common source of these local traditions to a date later than that of the Apostles, St. John dying within thirty or forty years of St. Justin's conversion and Tertullian's birth? Make what allowance you will for whatever possible exceptions can be taken to this representation; and then, after doing so, add to the concordant testimony of these two Fathers the evidence of St. Irenaeus, which is so close upon the School of St. John himself in

Asia Minor. "A three-fold cord", as the wise man says, "is not quickly broken." Only suppose there were so early and so broad a testimony, to the effect that our Lord was a mere man, the son of Joseph; should we be able to insist upon the faith of the Holy Trinity as necessary to salvation? Or supposing three such witnesses could be brought to the fact that a consistory of elders governed the local churches, or that each local congregation was an independent Church; or that the Christian community was without priests, could Anglicans maintain their doctrine that the rule of Episcopal succession is necessary to constitute a Church? And then recollect that the Anglican Church especially appeals to the ante-Nicene centuries, and taunts us with having superseded their testimony.

4. St.Cyril of Jerusalem (315-386)speaks for Palestine:

"Since through Eve, a virgin, came death, it behooved, that through a Virgin, or rather from a Virgin, should life appear; that, as the Serpent had deceived the one, so to the other Gabriel might bring good tidings."

-Cat. xii. 15.

5. St. Ephrem Syrus (he died 378) is a witness for the Syrians proper and the neighbouring Orientals, in contrast to the Graeco-Syrians. A native of Nisibis on the further side of the Euphrates, he knew no language but Syriac.

"Through Eve, the beautiful and desirable glory of men was extinguished; but it has revived through Mary."

-Opp. Syr. ii. p.318.

APPENDIX A

Again:

"In the beginning, by the sin of our first parents, death passed upon all men; today, through Mary we are translated from death unto life. In the beginning, the serpent filled the ears of Eve, and the poison spread thence over the whole body; today, Mary from her ears received the champion of eternal happiness: what, therefore, was an instrument of death, was an instrument of life also."

-iii. p.607.

6. St. Epiphanius (320-400) speaks for Egypt, Palestine, and Cyprus:

"She it is, who is signified by Eve, enigmatically receiving the appellation of the Mother of the living. It was a wonder that after the fall she had this great epithet. And, according to what is material, from that Eve all the race of man on earth is generated. But thus in truth from Mary the Life itself was born in the world, that Mary might bear living things, and become the Mother of living things. Therefore, enigmatically, Mary is called the Mother of living things.... Also, there is another thing to consider as to these women, and wonderful, as to Eve and Mary. Eve became a cause of death to men... and Mary a cause of life;... that life might be instead of death, life excluding death which came from the woman, viz. He who through the woman has become our life."

-Haer. 78. 18.

7. By the time of St. Jerome (331-420), the contrast between Eve and Mary had almost passed into a proverb. He says (Ep. xxii. 21, ad Eustoch.), "Death by Eve, life by Mary." Nor let it be supposed that he, any more than the preceding Fathers, considered the Blessed Virgin a mere physical instrument

APPENDIX A

of giving birth to our Lord, who is the Life. So far from it, in the Epistle from which I have quoted, he is only adding another virtue to that crown which gained for Mary her divine Maternity. They have spoken of faith, joy, and obedience; St. Jerome adds, what they had only suggested, virginity. After the manner of the Fathers in his own day, he is setting forth the Blessed Mary to the high-born Roman Lady, whom he is addressing, as the model of the virginal life; and his argument in its behalf is, that it is higher than the marriage-state, not in itself, viewed in any mere natural respect, but as being the free act of self-consecration to God, and from the personal religious purpose which it involves.

"Higher wage", he says, "is due to that which is not a compulsion, but an offering; for, were virginity commanded, marriage would seem to be put out of the question; and it would be most cruel to force men against nature, and to extort from them an angel's life."

-20

I do not know whose testimony is more important than St. Jerome's, the friend of Pope Damasus at Rome, the pupil of St. Gregory Nazianzen at Constantinople, and of Didymus in Alexandria, a native of Dalmatia, yet an inhabitant, at different times of his life, of Gaul, Syria, and Palestine.

8. St. Jerome speaks for the whole world, except Africa; and for Africa in the fourth century, if we must limit so world-wide an authority to place, witnesses St. Augustine (347-420). He repeats the words as if a proverb, "By a woman death, by a woman life" (Opp. t.v. Serm. 232); elsewhere he enlarges on the idea conveyed in it. In one place he quotes St. Irenaeus's words as cited above (adv. Julian i. n. 5). In another he speaks as follows:

Appendix A

> "It is a great sacrament that, whereas through woman death became our portion, so life was born to us by woman; that, in the case of both sexes, male and female, the baffled devil should be tormented, when on the overthrow of both sexes he was rejoicing; whose punishment had been small, if both sexes had been liberated in us, without our being liberated through both."
>
> -Opp. t. vi. De Agon. Christ. c.24.

9. St. Peter Chrysologus (406-450), Bishop of Ravenna, and one of the chief authorities in the 4th General Council:

> "Blessed art thou among women; for among women, on whose womb Eve, who was cursed, brought punishment, Mary, being blest, rejoices, is honoured, and is looked up to. And woman now is truly made through grace the Mother of the living, who had been by nature the mother of the dying.... Heaven feels awe of God, Angels tremble at Him, the creature sustains Him not, nature sufficeth not; and yet one maiden so takes, receives, entertains Him, as a guest within her breast, that, for the very hire of her home, and as the price of her womb, she asks, she obtains peace for the earth, glory for the heavens, salvation for the lost, life for the dead, a heavenly parentage for the earthly, the union of God Himself with human flesh."
>
> -Serm. 140.

It is difficult to express more explicitly, though in oratorical language, that the Blessed Virgin had a real meritorious co-operation, a share which had a "hire" and a "price", in the reversal of the fall.

10. St. Fulgentius, Bishop of Ruspe in Africa (468-533). The Homily which contains the following passage, is placed by Ceillier (t. xvi. p.127) among his genuine works:

"In the wife of the first man, the wickedness of the devil depraved her seduced mind; in the mother of the Second Man, the grace of God preserved both her mind inviolate and her flesh. On her mind it conferred the most firm faith; from her flesh it took away lust altogether. Since then man was in a miserable way condemned for sin, therefore without sin was in a marvellous way born the God-man."

-Senn. 2, p.124. De Dupi. Nati"

Such is which the Fathers have given us of Mary, as the Second Eve, the Mother of the living: I have cited ten authors. I could cite more, were it necessary: except the two last, they write gravely and without any rhetoric. I allow that the two last write in a different style, since the extracts I have made are from their sermons; but I do not see that the coloring conceals the outline. And after all, men use oratory on great subjects, not on small; nor would they, and other Fathers whom I might quote, have lavished their high language upon the Blessed Virgin, such as they gave to no one else, unless they knew well that no one else had such claims, as she had, on their love and veneration. (I p.33-46).

Appendix B

THERE IS AN OLD hermeneutical principle or called the "analogy of scripture" or the "analogy of faith," held by both orthodox Protestant biblical scholars and Catholic exegetes. By this principle or rule of interpretation the clear passages of Sacred Scripture lead the way to an understanding of the more obscure ones. The exegete, conscious of his or her faith, recognizes the intimate relationship between Scripture as Divine Revelation and the fixed truths of the Faith, and strives to explain Scriptural passages in such a way that the sacred writers will not be set in opposition to one another or to the revealed Faith. The Protestant biblical scholar R.C. Sproul (1939-2017) expressed the principle this way:

> If [Scripture] is the Word of God, it must therefore be consistent and coherent . . . [and] one may justly expect the entire Bible to be coherent, intelligible, and unified. Our assumption is that God, because of His omniscience, would never be guilty of contradicting Himself. It is therefore slanderous to the Holy Spirit to choose a particular passage that unnecessarily brings that passage into conflict with that which He has revealed elsewhere. So the governing principle of Reformed hermeneutics or interpretation is the analogy of faith.

Consistent with the principle of the analogy of Scripture is to understand certain Scriptural passages to refer to Mary in their larger meaning (because of the essential unity of God's revelation under the inspiration of the Holy Spirit) which do not name or even historically involve her. In the light of Genesis 3:15, *And I will*

Appendix B

put enmity between you and the woman, and between your offspring and hers; he will crush your head, and you will strike his heel, the several passages from the Old and New Testaments listed below seem to point to Mary expressly as the woman whose seed will crush the head of the serpent.

But it is of course Christ Who will crush the Serpent's head, not the woman *per se*; but it is the woman who is expressly said figuratively to be the Serpent's enemy.[1] The woman and her offspring are obviously intimately related and not only biologically. Hence, the woman is undoubtedly Mary; and the passages below, which clearly allude to the Genesis passage, refer to her. Although in each case, it is the woman (the church at Rome in the Romans passage) whose action, position, or posture analogously alludes to the crushing of the Serpent or defeat of Satan, and thus in each case typographically stands for Christ, she at the same time can be understood to refer to Mary (in the passage from John's Gospel it is historically Mary herself).

Jael kills Sisera with a tent stake through the head (Judges 4-5)

A woman drops a millstone on the skull of the traitor, Abimelech (Judges 9)

A wise woman arranges to have the rebel Sheba beheaded (2 Sam. 20)

Judith beheads Holofernes (Judith 13)

Esther causes Haman to be hung (Esther 7)

The "woman," the Mother of Jesus, is "standing" on Golgotha, the place of the skull" (John 21)

St. Paul tells the church at Rome that Satan is "under your feet" (Romans 16:20)

The "Great Sign": the Woman with the ruler of darkness "under her feet" (Revelation 12)

---

1. It is a common figure of speech (*metonymy*), to use a term that denotes one thing to refer to another, related thing, as when "eyes" are used to express or stand for the power of sight.

Bibliography

Aquinas, Saint Thomas. *Commentary on the Sentences of Peter Lombard*, 7-10. Edited by Peter Kwasniewksi and Jeremy Holmes. Translated by Beth Mortensen. Aquinas Institute.

———. "On the Hail Mary." Translated by Joseph B. Collins. https://thomasofaquino.blogspot.com/2015/08/on-hail-mary.html.

Augustine of Hippo, Saint. Sermons. *The Nicene and Post-Nicene Fathers.* Edited by Philip Schaff. Translated by Marcus Dodds. London: T & T Clark, 1900.

Blass and DeBrunner, *Greek Grammar of the New Testament and Other Early Christian Literature.* Translated and edited by Robert W. Funk. Chicago: University of Chicago Press, 1961.

Botterweck, Johannes G., Helmer Ringgren, and Heinz-Josef Fabry. *A Theological Dictionary of the Old Testament*, 10. Grand Rapids, MI: Wm. B. Eerdmans Publishing, 1977.

Calvin, John. *Calvini Opera*, 45. Berlin: Braunshweig, 1863-1900.

Campbell, Ted A. *Christian Confessions: A Historical Introduction.* Louisville, KY: Westminster John Knox Press, 1996.

Emmerich, Anne Catherine. *The Dolorous Passion of Our Lord Jesus Christ.* Charlotte, NC: Tan Books, 1983.

Epiphanius, "Ancoratus." *Patrologiae Cursus Completus. Series Latina*, 119. Edited by Jacques Paul Migne. Paris: Migne, 1844.

Gambero, Luigi. *Mary and the Fathers of the Church.* San Francisco: Ignatius Press, 1999.

Holweck, Frederick. "Candlemas." In *The Catholic Encyclopedia*, 3. New York: Robert Appleton Company, 1908.

Hunwicke, John. http://liturgicalnotes.blogspot.com/2016/08/assumptive-collects.html.

Lewis, C.S. *The Weight of Glory and Other Addresses.* Edited by Walter Hooper. New York: Macmillan, 1980.

Luther, Martin. *Weimar edition of Martin Luther's Works*, 11. Translated and edited by J. Pelikan St. Louis: Concordia, 1955.

Marshall, Taylor. "Did Jewish Temple Virgins Exist?" http://taylormarshall.com/2011/12/did-jewish-temple-virgins-exist-and-was.html.

Bibliography

McKim, Donald K. and Wright, David F., eds. *Encyclopedia of the Reformed Faith*. Louisville, KY: Westminster John Knox, 1992.

Newman, John Henry. *Mary: The Second Eve*, Eileen Breen, ed. Charlotte, NC: Tan Books, 1982.

———. *Certain Difficulties Felt by Anglicans in Catholic Teaching*. London: Longmans, Green & Co., 1896.

———. *A Letter to E. B. Pusey, D.D. on his Recent Eirenicon*. London: Longmans, Green & Co., 1866.

Phillipe, Marie-Dominique O.P. *Mystery of Mary*. Princeville, IL: The Congregation of St. John. Translated by Andre Faure-Beaulieu.

Pius IX, *Ineffabilis*. http://www.papalencyclicals.net/Pius09/p9ineff.htm.

Pusey, Eduard B. *An Eirenicon, In a Letter to The Author of "The Christian Year."* New York: Appleton & Co., 1866.

Ray, Steve. "Mary, the Ark of the New Covenant." https://www.catholic.com/magazine/print-edition/mary-the-ark-of-the-new-covenant.

Second Vatican Council, "Sacrosanctum Concilium," http://www.vatican.va/archive/hist_councils/ii_vatican_council/index.htm.

Thurston, Herbert. "Devotion to the Blessed Virgin Mary." *Catholic Encyclopedia.*, 15. New York: Robert Appleton Co., 1912.

Zwingli, Huldrych. *Zwingli Opera, Corpus Reformatorum* 1. Berlin, 1905.

www.ingramcontent.com/pod-product-compliance
Lightning Source LLC
Chambersburg PA
CBHW070455090426
42735CB00012B/2566